X MARKS THE BOX

DANIEL BLYTHE

X MARKS THE BOX

HOW TO MAKE POLITICS WORK FOR YOU

ICON BOOKS

Published in the UK in 2010 by
Icon Books Ltd, Omnibus Business Centre,
39–41 North Road, London N7 9DP
email: info@iconbooks.co.uk
www.iconbooks.co.uk

Sold in the UK, Europe, South Africa and Asia
by Faber & Faber Ltd, Bloomsbury House,
74–77 Great Russell Street,
London WC1B 3DA or their agents

Distributed in the UK, Europe, South Africa and Asia
by TBS Ltd, TBS Distribution Centre, Colchester Road,
Frating Green, Colchester CO7 7DW

Published in Australia in 2010
by Allen & Unwin Pty Ltd,
PO Box 8500, 83 Alexander Street,
Crows Nest, NSW 2065

Distributed in Canada by
Penguin Books Canada,
90 Eglinton Avenue East, Suite 700,
Toronto, Ontario M4P 2Y3

ISBN: 978-184831-051-3

Typeset in New Baskerville by Marie Doherty

Printed and bound in the UK by Clays Ltd, St Ives plc

*Politics is the art of looking for trouble, finding it whether
it exists or not, diagnosing it incorrectly, and applying
the wrong remedy.*
Ernest Benn (1875–1954)

About the Author

Daniel Blythe is a graduate of St John's College, Oxford. He is the author of several other books including the novels *The Cut* and *This is the Day* as well as the acclaimed *Encyclopaedia of Classic 80s Pop*. As well as writing, he leads creative writing workshops for adults, young people and children.

Author's Note

I would like to acknowledge the support given to me by a generous grant from the Authors' Foundation, without which this book could not have been completed. The Authors' Foundation is administered by the Society of Authors and more information can be found at the Society's website, www.societyofauthors.org.

Particular thanks go to: my agent Caroline Montgomery as ever, all the Icon editorial, publicity and sales team, and the many correspondents well-versed in the idiom of politics who were able to point me on the right path – but especially Steve Goddard, Iain Dale, Gisela Stuart, Jo-Anne Nadler, Peter Tatchell, Emma Jones and Angela Smith, who gave the most useful and considered answers to my niggling questions. Of course, any dissatisfaction with what follows should be laid entirely at my door!

Parliamentary material is reproduced with the permission of the Controller of HMSO on behalf of Parliament, and all quotes that are otherwise unattributed are from personal correspondence with the author.

Contents

1

Am I Bovvered? Politics for the disenchanted

The price good men pay for indifference to public affairs is to be ruled by evil men.
Plato (born c. 423 BC)

We are told that more people voted in the 2005 series of *Big Brother* than voted in the 2005 general election. Bearing in mind that old adage '85 per cent of statistics are made up', we should perhaps treat this piece of information with the scepticism it deserves. Many of the voters in *Big Brother* will have been teenage girls with their fingers permanently glued to the redial key on their mobiles – and, however imperfect British democracy may be, we haven't yet found any way of improving on the 'putting a cross in the box with a pencil' method. Furthermore, no matter how 'dumbed-down' people may accuse politics and the media of being, we have not yet sunk to the level of putting the candidates up for a Saturday night premium rate phone call challenge, with the decision between the final two remaining contenders being made by a bored Andrew Lloyd Webber or a merciless Simon Cowell.

Winston Churchill said that democracy was 'the worst form of government, except for all those other forms that have been tried from time to time'. This seems an elegant summation. You give people the chance to choose their own government – at least, to choose their own local Member of Parliament – and many of them can't be bothered. Actually, 39 per cent of them – that's the proportion who didn't bother to vote in 2005. Turnout dropped dramatically in the first decade of the new millennium with the 2001 and 2005 elections providing the smallest turnouts since the Second World War.

Now, we are being told politics is interesting again, and not just because of the credit crisis. But when the likes of *Big Brother* and *The X Factor* attract more young voters than the general election, something is clearly up. The British should be shamed by the electoral turnout in places like South Africa and Sierra Leone, where queues stretch round the block, and people need to bring water and small picnics to sustain them through the hours of waiting, and where voters, in between joining the queue and marking their cross, have been known to get married and divorced and give birth to children. (Not all of the above may be strictly true.)

So why are we so averse to politics? Later on in this book we'll examine some amusing attempts to 'sex up' politics, but for now we need to have a think about why people are so turned off it. Is it because we don't understand it? Is it because the polling booth is a half-mile walk away and *EastEnders* is on? Or, to misquote poet Adrian Mitchell, do most people ignore most politics because most politics ignores most people?

Some argue that the battle over the centre ground is just not interesting enough, with successive parties watering down their traditional policies in order to make themselves palatable to the electorate. Those who remember the 1980s will know that it was a fiery period for politics – in the Thatcher–Kinnock years, the Left and Right had hardly ever been more polarised. Now that the first decade of the twenty-first century has drawn to a close, though, those old distinctions start to look as if they are no longer applicable, with the two main parties agreeing on so much that the Liberal Democrats seem quite justified in claiming that, in many respects, they offer the radical alternative. Paradoxically, this comes at a time when the media have picked up the baton of a two-party debate again, and so the Lib Dems, with their ratings in the polls looking a little shaky under Nick Clegg, could find themselves squeezed out of the media narrative.

There is also some disengagement between what people vote for and what they get. Nobody actually voted for 'Tony Blair' or for 'Margaret Thatcher', apart from the few thousand constituents in Sedgefield and Finchley respectively. We all vote for the Member of Parliament who will represent our little corner of the country.

There are 646 constituencies, occasionally messed about with by order of the Boundary Commission, and at a general election or a by-election you go to vote for the member you want to speak up for your area, in theory. The party which gains the most Members is the largest in Parliament and is invited to form a government. Usually (although not always), the party forming the government will have an overall majority, meaning all their MPs add up to more than everybody else's put together.

The atmosphere in the House of Commons, especially during Prime Minister's Questions, is very much like that of the hubbub in a school assembly hall when the headmaster can't keep control. (You are not allowed to call anybody a liar in the House of Commons, but you can get away with *almost* anything else – we'll have a look at that later on.) The 1980s satire of the *Spitting Image* sketches, in which unruly MPs threw paper darts and apple cores, sometimes don't seem a huge exaggeration. So the ordinary voter could be forgiven for watching all this and wondering just what effect his or her cross in the box had. If you voted for the person who came second, it does not matter whether they lost by one single vote or 10,000 – it seems to count for nothing.

Let's take a look at the different types of voter and their motivation.

1. Bloody-Nosers

Some people make elections, local and national, into a way of commenting on the government's recent performance – they use them as a vote against the government rather than for anyone in particular. That's the oft-quoted 'bloody nose', such as that given to the Conservative administration of John Major, which lost ten successive by-elections in the 1990s and had a majority of 21 slowly whittled away over five years. Despite the nosebleeds, Major hung on, knowing he was going to lose and desperately hoping something would change for the better. (Harold Macmillan famously said that the greatest problem in politics was 'Events, dear boy', and these can work to a government's advantage, too.) Or there's that given to Labour in successive local elections in the first decade of the twenty-first century culminating in the absolute drubbing in 2008 which saw them relegated to third place behind the Liberal Democrats for the first time in decades. This was pretty embarrassing for them, especially as they generally go out of their way to pretend the Liberal Democrats don't exist.

Some voters take the idea rather too literally, such as the chap who swung a punch at John Prescott during the

2001 campaign (by far the most memorable incident of a duller-than-ditchwater election).

2. Single-Issuers

Never underestimate the power of the single-issue voter. Who can forget the 'Man in the White Suit', former BBC reporter Martin Bell, bestriding the constituency of Tatton in 1997 and giving the media one of those narratives they love to have during election campaigns? Bell stood as an 'anti-sleaze' independent candidate, and wrested the seat from the incumbent Conservative, Neil Hamilton, who had been associated with alleged corruption. Bell's victory condemned Hamilton and his terrifying wife to a career of promoting themselves in the media. And people often forget that, in the subsequent 2001 election, another single-issue candidate was elected, in the constituency of Wyre Forest – doctor-turned-politician Richard Taylor of Independent Community and Health Concern, who stood successfully on the ticket of saving the local hospital. (Successfully on the basis that he got elected, but sadly he didn't actually manage to save the hospital. One still has to admire him for trying.)

3. Diehards

There are places in the country where it is said, almost as folklore, that they don't count the Labour vote, they weigh it: Barnsley, for example. The same is true of the Tory vote in constituencies like Maidstone and Maidenhead. As yet, there is not really anywhere in the country which could describe itself as similarly 'safe' for the Liberal Democrats. (They have some seats with large majorities, but don't ever seem to take them for granted in quite the same way, possibly because the historical

precedent isn't as strong. The same is true for everybody
else, from the Greens down to the Monster Raving Loony
Party.)

It's in these 'safe' seats (although one could argue
that, post-1997, there isn't necessarily any such thing any
more – 'Labour Gain Hove', anyone?) that we encounter
the Diehard voter. Those whose grandfather and father
voted Labour/Tory and who would never dream of voting anything else. At least, that's what they *say*.

There's evidence of an emerging sub-species of
'grave-turners' – those who say: 'My dad/granddad would
turn in his grave *but* I'll be voting Labour/Tory this time
round.' They were seen in force at the 2008 Crewe and
Nantwich by-election – even railwaymen, who had sworn
to avenge the pillaging of their heritage and livelihood
by Thatcher by spitting in the general direction of the
Tories, found themselves lured back to the fold. History
will judge whether this was the turning point that David
Cameron's Conservatives claimed it was. What is generally accepted, though, is that a lot of previously reliable
Labour voters turned against Gordon Brown as a protest
against a number of issues and non-issues: the abolition
of the 10p tax rate, the rising cost of fuel, the generally
worse weather under Labour since 2007 … But were they
Diehards who had turned into Bloody-Nosers for one
by-election, or did it represent a significant shift of the
so-called 'C2' vote – Worcester Woman and Essex Man –
towards the Tories?

4. Floating voters

Those who don't know who to vote for. Or, more accurately, those who tell pollsters that they don't yet know
who they are going to vote for. A lot of people feel they

are 'floating voters' and are considering abstaining because they are aggrieved that none of the parties has really made much of an effort to court their vote. This seems reasonable, but betrays a misunderstanding of the way in which the parties distribute resources. Nobody is going to try very hard to win your vote unless you are in one of the key 100 or so constituencies on which the entire outcome of the general election will hinge.

The *Daily Mail's* impenetrably surreal cartoon 'Flook' once had weeks and weeks of strips around the running joke of the 'last floating voter' during the 1983 election, culminating in Flook (a strange bear-like creature) being chased by the political monsters (including a two-headed David Steel/David Owen) on polling day itself.

5. Zealots

The party faithful – the first at the polling station that morning, who will then spend the rest of the day on the streets, trying to tease voters out. They will already have spent the previous few weeks zipping around putting leaflets through doors and canvassing opinion on doorsteps. They usually have to resist the temptation to take up the offers of cups of tea, because: a) there is always the slight suspicion at the back of their minds that it's a delaying tactic by someone who intends to vote for the opposition, and who's been given instructions to waylay them by means of Earl Grey and shortbread biscuits, and b) the inevitable bladder crisis will rear its head after about three such stops, and there is nothing more likely to put someone off voting for their party than seeing someone in a blue/red/yellow/green rosette (delete as applicable) caught short by the roadside.

6. Tactical voters

How do you vote tactically? In a nutshell, a tactical vote is a vote *against* someone rather than *for* someone. It involves a situation where you would die before you would see the candidate from Party A getting into Parliament, but you are in a constituency where your preferred candidate, from Party B, does not have a snowflake's chance in hell of getting in. Therefore you transfer your allegiance, in name only, to Party C, who are in second place and therefore best placed to unseat the oleaginous chancer whose face you cannot bear to look at for a moment longer. The singer and activist Billy Bragg, well known as a Labour voter, has referred in public to voting tactically for the Liberal Democrats in the past. In some cities where neighbouring constituencies have different two-horse races (e.g. Labour/Lib Dem in one and Conservative/Lib Dem in another), voters make pacts to vote tactically for one another's parties, uniting against a common opponent.

7. The confused

Which is most of us, if we're honest.

Politics is shifting. If you grew up in the 1980s, you knew exactly where you were. The Tory government was led by a hectoring, resolute, steel-hearted woman who wanted to privatise everything, turn the UK into a giant American airbase and crush the unions, and the Labour opposition was led by a ginger Welshman with a propensity for falling over on beaches, supporting unilateral disarmament and losing elections. There was also a slightly comical third party led by two Davids, one of whom was actually taller than the other but was made to seem smaller by *Spitting Image*. You had the vague idea that Shirley Williams was in there somewhere too – they seemed a decent lot but, frankly, there was more chance of Bogchester Rovers winning the cup than of their ever holding power. And there was the Ecology party, an early incarnation of the Green party, who were painted as nutcases. Nobody would ever seriously advocate 'green' policies as a way of winning an election, would they? On the fringes, too, were the National Front. Nobody would ever take a bunch of right-wing racists seriously enough to interview them on the radio or treat them as a serious party, surely?

Fast-forward to the twenty-first century, and where are we? A nice young man with an earring and an open-necked shirt turns up on the doorstep, smiling and telling you he's in favour of getting more women, gay people and ethnic minorities into Parliament, engaging pupils with education, supporting the local state school, making the city a nuclear-free zone, being carbon neu-tral and saving the local hospital. You nod and say yes, you've always voted Labour so he can count on your sup-port. At this point his face falls, he pulls back his jacket to reveal the hitherto-concealed blue rosette and tells you in a somewhat pained voice that he is the Conservative party candidate.

Everyone is now squabbling over the centre ground. If your political allegiances were forged in the white heat of a decade in which political opinion was at its most polar-ised since the Second World War, you do find yourself struggling with this concept, and nodding sagely when-ever anyone quotes the old cliché that 'there's nothing to choose between the parties'.

That's not strictly true, of course – any MP, Parliamentary candidate or party activist worth their salt could give you, off the top of their head, five ways in which their party differs from the others. At least, they should be able to. But the *perception*, which is what matters, is increasingly that 'they're all the same'. At some point in the last fifteen years, every main party has elected a youngish, sharp-suited leader with an affable veneer, the air of a middle manager and a liking for matey banter, saying 'y'know' and strategically dropping aitches. Show a photograph of Nick Clegg to the man or woman in the street and a sizeable proportion of them will think he's David Cameron. (Show them a photograph of any other member of the Liberal Democrat front bench and they probably struggle to think anything at all, unless it's Lembit Opik, who's the only one most people can recognise because they may have seen him cavorting in *Hello* magazine with a Cheeky Girl.)

There is evidence that the parties are aware of the problem and that, whenever possible, the opposition does its best to put 'clear blue water' between them and the government, and vice versa. The water is inevitably muddied, though, by the presence of rebels on both sides – the Iraq war, tuition fees and the abolition of the 10p tax rate being just some examples in recent years of votes where the force of the Labour rebels threatened to defeat the government.

Also, there's a fair point often made by opposition parties, which is that it isn't reasonable to expect them to present clear, committed breakdowns of their tax plans when an election might still be years away. That sort of thing should be in a manifesto, and you can take them to task if it's not.

8. Spoilers

One way of indicating your lack of engagement in the political process is actively to mark your paper in some way other than the traditional X, or other sign of 'unambiguous intent', to quote the voting regulations. This can range from writing 'IDIOTS' or 'WASTE OF SPACE' next to every candidate's name to scrawling 'COME THE REVOLUTION YOU'LL BE FIRST AGAINST THE WALL' across the entire ballot slip. This might all at first sound rather childish, but a spoilt paper has to be counted. Parliamentary election rules (Schedule 1 to the Representation of the People Act 1983) stipulate that 'public notice' must be given of the number of rejected ballot papers. This is usually taken to mean given in writing, but such notice may also be given as part of the announcement of the results by the returning officer. There are corresponding rules for local elections. A large number of spoilt ballots in any one constituency might send out a message about the weakness or unpalatability of the selection of candidates on offer.

Of course, you may end up kicking yourself if someone wins by two votes. The seat of Winchester, in the 1997 election, was won by Mark Oaten for the Liberal Democrats with a majority of two. The defeated Conservative, Gerry Malone, successfully challenged the result on a technicality and a by-election was called – which Oaten won with a majority of 21,556. (It would be satisfying to say that Oaten had the last laugh, although his enforced resignation from the Lib Dems' Home Office brief a few years later, after admitting shenanigans with male escorts, rather prevents one from doing so.)

9. Splitters

A particular sub-category of Spoilers (and a spoilt ballot
is how it is counted) like to make their views known by
marking a cross against more than one candidate having been instructed not to do so. The Glasgow East by-
election in 2008 apparently had a number of spoilt papers
on which people had marked both the Labour and the
SSP (Scottish Socialist Party) candidate. Confusion, or
divided loyalties? Things may have been confused further by the fact that the two candidates shared a surname
(Margaret Curran and Frances Curran). Splitting does
no actual good beyond enabling you to square things
with your conscience – there's no such thing as half a
vote – so it's up to you.

10. Abstainers

Not voting – is it the coward's way? The only problem
is that, unless people 'actively abstain' (by spoilt ballot),
there is no way of telling the difference between a) the
high-minded, who wish to keep their political fingers
clean by not allowing their pencil to sully the box of any
of the reprobates on offer, b) the disillusioned, who dis-
trust not just the candidates on offer but the entire political system, c) the lazy, who are aware there is an election
happening but would rather put their feet up in front of
Coronation Street and d) the ignorant, who haven't got a
clue what's going on and wonder if people are walking
around with rosettes on for a horse show. They all count
as a non-vote, all contributing towards the 39 per cent,
or whatever it turns out to be, of the population who are
cited as not voting. So the best way of doing it is to be a
Spoiler – see above.

So there we have it. Chances are you'll have been in one of the above categories, or you're about to get the vote and wondering which you will fall into. So where will your vote go?

Who are they? The political parties in the UK

Labour

In government since 1997, having won a record three consecutive terms. Founded in 1900, having grown out of the trade union and socialist movements, and traditionally regarded as the party on the left of British politics – although Tony Benn and others would have a few words to say about that these days. Two long periods of opposition in the twentieth century (1951–64 and 1979–97) resulted in a lot of soul-searching, and the party now represents a more centrist, social-democratic position. Since 2008, it could be argued that Labour has become even friendlier towards big business, and many long-term supporters feel the party has betrayed its roots. It has not taken long for initial excitement with Labour to turn to disenchantment.

Conservative

Known as the Tory party, and also the subject of a period of redefinition following a bruising extended period in opposition. Founded in the nineteenth century and traditionally a right-wing party, it could now be seen as centre-right. They are in an odd position, ideologically – what some see as support for individualism and the fight against the 'nanny state' others see as being out of touch and wanting to maintain the status quo at the expense of progress. Struggling to shake off the spectre of Thatcherism, the party has adopted policies which

would have been unthinkable in the 1980s: an engagement with poverty and social division, and open support
for civil partnerships. But some commentators feel the
disagreements on Europe which plagued John Major in
the 1990s have not gone away, and could come back to
haunt a future Conservative administration.

Liberal Democrats

Until the 1920s, the Liberal party was one of the two
major parties in British politics, but it was eased out by
the rise of Labour. A Liberal party, in some form, traditionally occupied the centre ground of British politics
throughout the rest of the twentieth century. The Liberal
Democrats were formed out of the former SDP/Liberal
alliance in 1988. Continually frustrated by the media portraying UK politics as a two-horse race, and often struggling for airtime, the 'Lib Dems' have nevertheless made
some bold advances. They always tend to do better in
local and European elections – and in by-elections – than
in general elections. Their supporters would say their
centrist position encourages support from both Left and
Right and, indeed, that they want to erode those old
definitions and 'isms' – their detractors would claim that
they attract equal hostility from both sides!

And it's only fair to mention a few of the others.

The next biggest in terms of seats is the Democratic
Unionist Party, founded by the shy and retiring Reverend
Ian Paisley, which wants to maintain the cultural ties
between Northern Ireland and Great Britain. Fifth biggest
is the Scottish Nationalist Party, which does what it says on
the tin – it wants independence for Scotland. Devolution
appears to have gone part of the way towards keeping the
latter happy, but their MPs still sit in Westminster. Sinn

Féin is the major left-wing Irish Republican party. Plaid Cymru stands for the establishment of an independent Welsh state within the European Union, and has a handful of MPs. The UK Independence Party currently has no representation at Westminster and sports possibly one of the least imaginative of all party logos, featuring a pound symbol on a plain background with the party name, but has had eloquent spokesmen in Nigel Farage and subsequently in Lord Pearson. Respect is a coalition created in 2004 out of issues around the Iraq conflict, and has since broadened its remit, while the Green Party has members in the European Parliament and the London Assembly, and have been poised for a while to take their first Westminster seat. Putting it all into perspective is the Official Monster Raving Loony Party, standing, in its own words, for 'Insanity, Satire, Pragmatism, Existentialism'.

Here is one possible wording for a sticky label for ballot papers, suggested by the 'Abstain 05' campaign during the 2005 general election: 'This vote is an abstention. I deeply mistrust the current political system such that I cannot cast a vote today in favour of a particular candidate and I am therefore abstaining. This should be a wake-up call for all politicians who think they can treat the electorate in the way they have done over the past few years or more. I will continue to abstain until I feel I can again trust one or more of the political leaders.'*

---

* Abstain 05 campaign website: http://www.abstain05.co.uk/

None of the Above?

There is an argument for a 'none of the above' or NOTA choice – or indeed the RON (Re-Open Nominations) so beloved of student councils, although the administrative headache a victory for this category would produce hardly bears thinking about. Never mind the confusion which could arise if there actually was a candidate called Ron. And how many people would actually trudge through the pouring rain to their local polling station just to say that none of the options on offer was any good? And what would happen if NOTA got the most votes?

If you really do find all the proffered candidates unpalatable, here are a few suggestions from some useful sources.

- The campaign 'Positive Abstention' lobbies for positive abstention votes to be included on ballot papers and in election statistics. This may appeal to you. (www.positiveabstention.com)
- Emma Jones, a Haringey councillor, thinks you can always find an option: 'There will always be one candidate or party that is closer to your own beliefs than the others, even if only slightly – and not voting for them of course helps the others with whom you have less in common. Or the other option is to stand as a candidate yourself, perhaps as an Independent – but if you cannot or don't want to do that, don't moan about the people who are giving up their life to do so.'
- Iain Dale, Conservative activist and blogger, argues that: 'If someone doesn't vote they have no right to complain about what happens afterwards.'

- Similarly, Gisela Stuart MP says: 'If you don't vote, politicians don't have to care!'
- Peter Tatchell, human rights campaigner, suggests you should: 'Write on the ballot paper "None of the above".'
- Anyone who can't bring themselves to vote for any of the candidates on offer should 'put themselves up for election next time!', says writer and journalist Jo-Anne Nadler.

The words 'None of the Above' as part of a political party name are prohibited under the Registration of Political Parties (Prohibited Words and Expressions) (Amendment) Order 2005. So currently, nobody can actually stand as the candidate for the 'None of the Above' party.

With all of these potential coping strategies in evidence, it's perhaps surprising that so many people chose to 'abstain passively'. Why do people not vote? Unsurprisingly, there has been some serious research done into this. After the 2005 general election, a poll of non-voters found that 13 per cent were 'very interested', in politics, 43 per cent were 'interested', 30 per cent were 'not particularly interested' and 14 per cent were 'not at all interested'. Intriguingly, though, these non-voters still professed the same concerns as the rest of the population – crime, health, money and so on – but they just didn't necessarily see this abstract thing called 'politics' as being the answer to their problems.[*]

---

[*] MORI survey for the Electoral Commission, 2005: http:// ukpollingreport.co.uk/blog/archives/date/2006/07

So, with only a minority of non-voters actually appearing not to take an interest in politics, there must be something else turning them off. The same poll also asked people's reasons for not voting, of which the largest group (19 per cent) was the 'not bothered' group, followed by 13 per cent who expressed a lack of trust in politicians and 9 per cent who claimed a lack of choice.[*]

You may be one of these people. You may well be looking at the politicians who supposedly represent you and wondering what on earth they can possibly have to say that would be of any use. Well, read on – with any luck the subsequent chapters will help to bring home all the weird and wonderful things which politics *can* be about and which it *can* do for you.

PolFax: Day By Day

- Most people think UK elections are always held on a Thursday, and indeed they now are, but that hasn't always been the case.
- The 1931 election, held in the middle of the Great Depression, took place on a Tuesday.
- Wednesday was the day of choice in 1922 and 1924.
- Election day was a Saturday in 1918 (the first election in which women could vote). A regional newspaper noted: 'Polling on Saturday was conducted very quietly and there was an entire absence of the usual excitement. Weather had its effect on polling for out of 2,400 persons entitled to record these votes

---

[*] Ibid.

only about 1,500 did so. The majority of these were women. Polling took place in the Parish Hall."*

- In many countries – France, for example – elections are held on a Sunday so as not to disrupt work and schools.

- The timing of elections remains a controversial issue, with an incumbent prime minister currently able to call one at any time within the maximum five-year period of a Parliament.

- In 2007, Labour's deputy leader Harriet Harman argued that a PM should be forced to seek majority approval from MPs when choosing a date.

- The Liberal Democrat MP David Howarth has gone further still, leading a campaign for fixed-term Parliaments.[†]

- Tuesday is traditionally the day for the prime minister's audience with the monarch, it's Wednesday for Prime Minister's Questions, and most MPs have their constituency surgeries on a Saturday.

The Numbers Game: Close Shaves

Parliamentary majorities of less than ten votes since 1918

MP	Party	Constituency	Year	Majority
Abraham Flint	Nat Lab	Ilkeston	1931	2
Mark Oaten	Lib Dem	Winchester	1992	2[‡]
Sir Francis Acland	Lib	Tiverton	1923	3
Gwynoro Jones	Lab	Carmarthen	1974 (February)	3

---

* *East Grinstead Observer*, 21 December 1918.
† Fixed Term Parliaments Bill, *Hansard* 16 May 2008: Column 1703.
‡ Later declared void, but subsequently won in a by-election by the Liberal Democrats with a 21,556 majority.

MP	Party	Constituency	Year	Majority
Sir Harmar Nicholls	Con	Peterborough	1966	3
Thomas Stamford	Lab	Leeds West	1924	3
Lord Colum Crichton-Stuart	Con	Northwich	1929	4
Hon. George Ward	Con	Worcester	1945	4
Eric Gandar Dower	Con	Caithness and Sutherland	1945	6
Leonard Ropner	Con	Sedgefield	1923	6
Dennis Hobden	Lab	Brighton Kemptown	1964	7
Frank Privett	Con	Portsmouth Central	1922	7
Derek Spencer	Con	Leicester South	1983	7
Paul Tyler	Lib	Bodmin	1974 (February)	9

Vox Pops

The first election under the Ballot Act has been throughout peaceful. Persons of great experience declare that they never saw a contested election in which less intoxicating liquor was drunk. No charges of bribery are rife, and the election appears to have been fought on both sides on principles of purity.

Report from *The Times*, 16 August 1872, after the first ever secret ballot in the UK

One of the penalties for refusing to participate in politics is that you end up being governed by your inferiors.

Plato (born c. 423 BC)

2

Push the Vote Out: Democracy in action

You turn if you want to. The lady's not for turning.
Margaret Thatcher (British prime minister 1979–90)

I didn't get into government to do the safe and easy things.
A ship in harbour is safe, but that's not why the ship is built.
Sarah Palin (US vice-presidential candidate, 2008)

Setting the date

A general election in the UK has to be called within five years and one month of the last one. However, in practice this has varied hugely, at least since the Second World War. 1974 saw two elections, with Harold Wilson scraping home in February and clinging on until he was re-elected in October. Some people thought James Callaghan would go to the country in October 1978, but he made the fatal error of waiting until May 1979 (and even then it was only because his hand was forced by a vote of no confidence). Mrs Thatcher favoured four-year Parliaments with spring elections, as did Tony Blair – while John Major hung on desperately between 1992 and 1997 in the hope that something, somewhere would happen to boost his flagging poll ratings. He may have been hoping for a miracle.

One of the funniest – and indeed saddest – things about politics is the sight of political leaders being interviewed and having to smile confidently and say: 'Yes, of course we're going to win, and win well,' when you know that what's going through their head is, 'We're going to lose. This idiot asking the question knows that, the public watching know it, so who am I trying to kid?' It can be a damage limitation exercise, of course. If you start saying you are going to lose, you risk your core vote not turning out and you end up losing even some of the seats you'd been sure of hanging on to – thus making things ten times worse for the unfortunate who then has to take over as leader of the opposition for four years.

The government of the time can manipulate the election date to their best advantage, as seen most clearly in 2007 by the infamous autumn 'non-election', which Gordon Brown was forced to deny by calling in what an ITV reporter rather caustically called a 'tame journalist' (the BBC's Andrew Marr) for the sole purpose of declaring that no, after all, he wasn't going to call an election. It's hard to imagine this happening in any other sphere of life: David Bowie calling a press conference to announce that he's not releasing a new album or going on tour for the next two years, or Martin Amis being interviewed on BBC4 to make it clear that he won't be having a new novel published any time in the near future. So, we had the spectacle of Gordon rebuking everyone for this silly speculation, which of course was distracting the media when the PM just wanted to 'get on with running the country'. (This has been quite a refrain of the twilight years of New Labour, whenever they want to deflect discussion of awkward topic: 'People aren't interested in X, they just want us to get on with running the country.' The public, of course, would perhaps like the chance to say they want someone *else* running the country.)

The whole thing seems quite unfair, given that the government can have the election when they want it, unless they keep hoping and just run out of time like John Major did in 1997.

There is an alternative. Liberal Democrat MPs David Heath and David Howarth have been campaigning for the UK to have fixed-term Parliaments, tabling a bill to this effect (it failed at the second reading in May 2008). The campaign had the support of former Lib Dem leader Sir Menzies Campbell, who said: 'It's now generally accepted that it's quite wrong that it should be within the discretion of the prime minister to decide when he wants a general election.'* And indeed, why not? America does it, knowing that every other even-numbered year there will be a race for the White House – while we still sit in uncertainty as each Parliament chugs on, not knowing if it will be derailed by knife-wieldings and resignations, or be stretched to the absolute limit by hope in adversity (for example, the Conservative government between 1992 and 1997). A poll in 2007 indicated that 44 per cent of all MPs support fixed-term Parliaments and 49 per cent oppose them, which is a pretty good support base to start from.[†]

The case against is that the media love a narrative, and having the 'milestone' of a fixed election date would bowl them a very easy ball. The fixed cut-off date of a general election could also take away the impetus from any policies formulated in the year running up to the election date, which would risk alienating voters even

---

* Interview with Jon Sopel on *The Politics Show*, BBC1, Sunday 7 October 2007.

† '44 per cent of MPs support fixed term Parliaments', posted on http://www.fixedterm.org.uk on 27 December 2007. Pollsters ComRes interviewed 154 MPs in October 2007.

further. No straightforward answers, then. Take a look at www.fixedterm.org.uk and have your say.

> *Whilst the current system generally favours the incumbent, we would have other problems with fixed terms, i.e. that once past halfway through the term we would be back into electioneering again.*
>
> Jo-Anne Nadler, writer and journalist

Naming the day

The last seven general elections have all been held at some time in the second quarter of the year. There is sensible thinking behind this. Governments don't tend to go for autumn or (heaven help us) winter elections if they can possibly help it. Who is going to turn out for an election in a howling gale or a hailstorm? It's hard enough to get people off their backsides in the summer. It also makes sense to combine the polling with that for city council and borough council elections, which happen in May.

There is an interesting theory – put about during the media buzz in autumn 2007, when Brown was dithering – that an autumn election favours the Tories. Why? Because short days and dark nights make working people trudging home for tea less inclined to vote, and favour those who have time to venture out in the grey winter light of day. This theory seems to be born of some long-lost, mythical Albion in which all those of a Conservative persuasion spend their days idly quaffing brandy, polishing expensive cars on gravel drives and working out the best ways to exploit their domestic staff, while all left-wing voters are calloused-palmed, ragged-trousered, salt-of-the-earth, flat-capped manual labourers slogging home after an honest day's toil at the coalface. Where this leaves the Lib Dems – who presumably, in this world-view, all eat tofu, wear big woolly jumpers and sandals, and work for universities or in the voluntary sector – is anybody's guess.

Whenever it happens to be, go out and vote. Find out when the polling booths are open – it will say on your polling card when it comes through the door – and make sure you get down there and register your vote. Even if it's at 9.45pm, in the pouring rain and the dark.

Some activists like to offer lifts to the polling station for people who have difficulty getting out and about. Obviously, they hope to be doing this only for their own supporters, but they have to take people on trust ... Would anyone deliberately waste the time of a Labour activist with a car on polling day by filling it up with 'housebound' Conservatives? One fears they would.

Doing it right?

Young people aren't averse to voting. They like voting. In fact, they love it. They find it exciting, hang on the results with enormous anticipation and discuss them in colleges, universities and youth clubs up and down the land. It's just a shame that this zeal for *Big Brother* and *The X Factor* doesn't transfer into the political arena.

Why should this be the case? Millions of people on Friday and Saturday nights – admittedly not as many millions as a few years ago, but still a hell of a lot – are enthused by a bunch of wannabes who are either bickering, flirting and performing the daftest of tasks in a minimalist surrealist show home, 24 hours a day, or belting out Gloria Gaynor covers to a karaoke backing track while bedecked in excessive mascara and make-up (and that's just the boys).

One thing's for sure – politicians and reality TV don't mix. People still shudder at the memory of George Galloway on *Celebrity Big Brother*, furthering the cause of the Respect party's agenda by dressing in a red lycra catsuit and lapping milk from a bowl held by Rula Lenska. And yet politicians still toy with the idea of using this medium to get their message across – as early as 2002, Argentina was piloting a programme called *The People's Candidate*, in which a candidate for national legislative elections would be chosen by a *Big Brother*-style vote. The programme *American Candidate*, which ran in the USA alongside the 2004 presidential elections, seemed to have loftier ambitions – it aimed to put unknown candidates and their policies on primetime TV, and to get the public to vote for them until all bar one had been eliminated. The winner, a conservative Christian candidate with a frightening bouffant hairdo and a beatific manner, saw the contest primarily as 'a tremendous opportunity to be a witness for Christ'.*

Perhaps the best legacy of this 'reality TV' approach to politics is the tendency towards interactivity in political media now – for example, the fact that programmes such as *Question Time* invite viewer participation via text message. Here are some interesting turnout facts:

• 66 per cent of people who did not vote in 2005 would have voted if online voting had been available – bear in mind the context, though, of this research, namely

---

* *New York Times*, 12 October 2004.

that it was undertaken by YouGov on behalf of IT
company Cisco Systems.*

- Local council elections have worse turnouts than general elections – recent turnout in England has been
as low as one in three eligible voters.†
- Postal ballots have been trialled in some local elections, with some figures suggesting that it pushed
turnout up to 40 per cent, well above the level
expected.‡

Is walking to a polling booth, picking up a stub of pencil
which is tied to the wall, and marking a cross on a piece
of paper not a woefully archaic method of voting in the
internet age? Would the chance to register one's vote
online not improve turnout dramatically? Well, yes and
no. Arguments have been made for it being potentially
discriminatory, and the Security Peer Review Group, a
US panel of experts in computerised election security,
concluded in 2007 that internet-based voting systems
would also pose 'a serious and unacceptable risk' of election fraud,§ a concern shared by the UK Electoral Reform
Society.¶

There is a lot to be said for an 'if it ain't broke, don't
fix it' mentality, and, while a turnout of around 60 per
cent using the old-fashioned paper-and-pencil method is
far from being ideal, it is well short of disastrous. It has to
be borne in mind that turnout goes up when an election

---

* Cited in 'Brits want to vote online, dammit', 20 July 2005: http://
www.theregister.co.uk/2005/07/20/brits_want_to_vote/
† *Daily Telegraph*, 28 April 2008.
‡ Ben Russell, 'ELECTIONS 2004: Postal ballot a "triumph" as 40%
take part', *Independent*, 11 June 2004.
§ www.servesecurityreport.org
¶ 'What Is E-Voting?' at www.electoral-reform.org.uk

is seen as being close (witness 1992), and drops if the result seems to be a foregone conclusion – despite their problems, it would have been a huge surprise if Labour had been in danger of losing the elections of 2001 and 2005. The future is an entirely different matter, with experts expecting turnout to go up as the parties' poll positions grow tighter.

Something else which may inspire you is going to see the House of Commons for yourself.

If you want to see Prime Minister's Questions, all you need to do is write to your MP's office requesting a ticket. They have a limited allocation for the year, but if you live outside London you may have more of a chance. At the St Stephen's Entrance to the House of Commons you'll be given a laminated pass which you then show as you pass through a security check, and these days it's all pretty tight – you walk through a metal detector and you'll be asked by some burly gentlemen to hand over bags and coats to be scanned as well. There's usually quite a wait in the Central Lobby and on the stairs, even when you already have a ticket, so it's a good idea to get there early – Prime Minister's Question Time (PMQs) takes place at 12.30 and arriving before noon is advisable.

You'll be asked, in the cloakrooms outside the public gallery of the Commons, to leave behind your camera, mobile phone and so on. And then you proceed into some seats on a precipitous slope, like the highest gallery of a theatre. Below you, on the other side of a sheet of strengthened glass, you'll be able to see the assembled MPs – or, at least, those who are sitting far enough forward for you to see them. It gives the impression of being cramped, despite the lofty ceiling. Across the Chamber you'll be able to see the other galleries, including the press gallery where the seasoned hacks loll, pens poised. Despite the screening-off, the sense of anticipation is palpable, and whoever the prime minister of the day is, there is a buzz when he (or she!) comes into the Chamber.

Two big plasma screens on either side of the glass will display events, and you'll have an order paper showing you the business of the day. You'll have a good view of the wooden dispatch boxes which are used as lecterns by the prime minister (on your left) and the leader of the opposition (on your right).

With any luck you may get a lively debate. When I visited I was lucky in my choice of day, as it was a rollicking session, with Gordon Brown on the ropes over the abolition of the 10p tax rate and the teachers' strike, and facing David Cameron's favourite exhortation to 'be straight with people'. Outside, the demonstrators demanding an English Parliament could not be ignored. But the session goes by incredibly quickly – it only lasts half an hour, and only since 1997 has it been one half-hour Wednesday session as opposed to two quarter-hour sessions on a Tuesday and a Thursday – and many visitors come away with a vague feeling of disappointment. Once a week, the grandstanding, gladiatorial contest is what gets the most attention – it's theatre, and to some extent the participants know this.

John McEnroe, in his showpiece seniors' matches, shouts: 'You cannot be serious!' at the umpire because it's expected, and Bruce Springsteen knows he's expected to play 'Born in the USA'. In the same way, PMQs has its 'greatest hits' as well. At some point, there will be a toadying question from a backbencher – something along the lines of: 'Would my right honourable friend agree with me that my constituency, which was a depressed

wasteland in 1997, is now the centre of a cultural revolution thanks to this government's instigation of free entry
to museums and art galleries?' – and this will receive the
obligatory jeers from the opposition. The valiant leader
of the Liberal Democrats, whoever he is this week, will
struggle to make himself heard above the barracking
from both sides. And at some point, someone will mention 'the bad old days of boom and bust', which will get a
rousing cheer. (They tend not to do that one any more,
for obvious reasons.) And all the worthy work which goes
on behind the scenes in smaller, more measured debates
and committees doesn't get any attention at all, even
though it's all there to watch on BBC Parliament.

One cannot help feeling let down – the sense of distance, and of dividing 'us' from 'them' with the glass par-
tition, is palpable. If you're lucky, you may get to collar
one or two MPs in the lobby afterwards, but they won't
stop to chat for long.

X Marks the …

However, you can tell when a general election campaign
is under way, as your MP suddenly starts being a *lot* more
visible and vocal. He or she, along with those who would
take his or her seat, starts sending you several forests'
worth of photocopied or glossy leaflets through the door.
These are always very amusing, as they go out of their way
to play with statistics to pretend that their party – whether
they are Labour, Conservative, Liberal Democrat, Green,
Socialist Worker, Communist, UKIP or Monster Raving
Loony – is the only one with a fighting chance in the constituency, and that you'd be wasting your time with any of
the others. They will invariably feature the candidate in

a variety of interesting poses, and will try to mention his name more times than is decently necessary.

Let's say your local candidate of a certain political colour is called Jeremy Wannabe. The leaflet will have JEREMY WANNABE in big letters at the top, the first article will feature Parliamentary candidate Jeremy Wannabe visiting a local school and grinning beside the school sign with parents, while the next will feature Jeremy Wannabe frowning in concern and puzzlement next to some graffiti. There may even be a before/after shot, with Jeremy Wannabe frowning at the graffiti in the first shot and proudly brandishing a cloth and some cleaning fluid beside a scrubbed-clean (possibly Photoshopped) wall in the next. The leaflet will be peppered with quotes from Jeremy Wannabe, and some statistics on local crime figures will be, depending on Jeremy's relationship with the government, effusively praised as a triumph for local investment in policing resources or scathingly denounced as proof of the breakdown of law and order on your doorstep. Finally, there may be a comment on a new resource for children, young people or old people in your area – and, to get the lowdown on this, they will have cast the net far and wide and canvassed the views of Parliamentary candidate Jeremy Wannabe.

This may sound like overkill, but it is all part of the game. Getting the candidate's name out there is half the battle – if they have a memorable name, so much the better. It's even been argued that a candidate whose surname falls in the first half of the alphabet gains an advantage (candidates are listed alphabetically on ballot slips).

If you get the chance to question the candidate in person, it is always a good idea to do so. Even if they may not immediately have an answer to your question, it's good to put them on the spot and make them think about issues which they may not yet have covered, or on which they may not yet have all the information to hand. There will be various ways of doing this:

Hustings – a public debate involving one or more of the candidates

Radio – the chances are that the candidates will do a radio slot, and this may involve phone-in questions from the listeners

Canvassing – yes, you may just get the chance to interrogate the candidate on your very doorstep. They'll be there to get a sense of whether you'll vote for them, but ignore that – that's what *they* want. You should get what *you* want out of those few minutes, and pin them down with some exacting questions. They may not agree with you, and may think what you ask of them is quite bizarre. Fair enough – it's one thing going out there to solicit votes, but it's quite another being prepared to do anything and everything one's constituents demand.

Power to the People

Cynics would claim that politicians are on to a good thing here – people's participation in the democratic process is reduced to marking one box on a voting slip in a shabby hall every four or five years. Of course, the cynics aren't always right. This view ignores people's chance to take part in local and council elections, and there are far more ways of participating in what's broadly called 'politics' than simply voting.

If you don't like something the government of the time is doing, you don't just have to sit tight and wait five years until you get to vote them out. You can always walk up and down waving a placard – as long as you don't do it within a certain distance of the Houses of Parliament, of course, and definitely not anywhere near the steel barriers. You can heckle the prime minister – but you won't get further than the gates at the end of Downing Street. You can barrack speakers at a party conference – until you get removed by the heavies. And you can write to your MP – although if they're a government MP, you may only get a form response back, stapled to a wad of policy summaries.

In fact, those cynics may well have a case after all.

PolFax: The PM Hit Parade

In 1999, BBC Radio 4 asked a panel of prominent historians, politicians and commentators to rank the prime ministers of the previous 100 years, from best to worst. (Tony Blair was excluded from the poll, being still in office.) These were the results:

1. Winston Churchill (Con, 1940–45 and 1951–55)
2. David Lloyd George (Lib, 1916–22)
3. Clement Attlee (Lab, 1945–51)
4. Herbert Henry Asquith (Lib, 1908–16)
5. Margaret Thatcher (Con, 1979–90)
6. Harold Macmillan (Con, 1957–63)
7. Robert Cecil, 3rd Marquess of Salisbury (Con, 1885–86, 1886–92, 1895–1902)
8. Stanley Baldwin (Con, 1923–24, 1924–29, 1935–37)

9. Sir Henry Campbell-Bannerman (Lib, 1905–08)
10. Harold Wilson (Lab, 1964–70, 1974–76)
11. Edward Heath (Con, 1970–74)
12. James Callaghan (Lab, 1976–79)
13. Andrew Bonar Law (Con, 1922–23)
14. Ramsay MacDonald (Lab, 1924, 1929–31, 1931–35)
15. Alec Douglas-Home (Con, 1963–64)
16. Arthur Balfour (Con, 1902–05)
17. John Major (Con, 1990–97)
18. Neville Chamberlain (Con, 1937–40)
19. Anthony Eden (Con, 1955–57)

Vox Pops

I don't spend my nights in the Cologne sewage plant, so why should I let myself get interviewed by Der Spiegel?

Helmut Kohl (German chancellor, 1982–98), offering his robust views on the press.

3

Poll Position: Election fever

War is nothing more than the continuation of policy by other means.
Carl Philipp Gottlieb von Clausewitz (1780–1831),
Prussian soldier and military theorist

Never Mind The Ballots

It is fair to say that certain general election campaigns of the past have caught the public imagination more than others. Whether because of public interest in particular characters, the stability of the political or economic situation at the time, or simply the weather (yes, the weather), some of these rare events have simply been particularly memorable. Here's a run-down of the best five from recent years – and then a brief look at the biggest damp squib of the lot.

June 1970

It was the first general election held after the 1969 Representation of the People Act, and therefore it was the first in which those aged eighteen to twenty were eligible to vote. We take it for granted, now, that politicians go around seeking the 'yoof' vote and are desperate to court teenagers who will (perhaps) be casting their first ballot in the election to come. The various attempts to woo the *Big Brother*-watching demographic have their origins in this election.

This one was a surprise. Ted Heath's Conservatives, derided by Labour as 'Yesterday's Men', came back into power, knocking out a government with a workable majority for the first and only time since the Second World War.

Those who grew up in the 1970s and were even vaguely aware of the news believed that the pendulum of British politics swung back and forth every few years, which was perhaps partly why growing up under a decade of Thatcherism came as such a shock to many young people.

There are various amusing theories about the factors which brought about Wilson's unexpected 1970 defeat, including one relating to the England football team's poor performance in the 1970 World Cup in Mexico having a knock-on effect on the government. (Again, we see echoes of this in later years; Tony Blair, it is rumoured, closely watched the England side's performance at their World Cup qualifiers in the run-up to 1997.) The campaign itself did not catch fire, perhaps because of distractions in Mexico, but 1970 is included here as an important milestone.

February 1974

It seems odd these days for the leader of the losing party not to resign immediately. Harold Wilson didn't – he sat out four years in opposition before making this dramatic, if precarious, comeback in 1974. For the first time since the Second World War, the UK had a hung parliament, in which no party held an overall majority. Ted Heath's Conservatives actually won the most votes, but lost the support of the Ulster Unionists, and so 'man of the people' Wilson began his attempt to become prime minister for a second time.

The slogan Heath had run with was: 'Who governs Britain?' – a bad idea as it obviously invited the response: 'Well, not you, thanks very much.'

Immortalised in the public consciousness by comedian Mike Yarwood's pipe-smoking impression of him, Wilson was not averse to expanding his media profile elsewhere after his 1976 resignation – he had his own David Frost-style chat show for a while. The mind boggles a) at the idea of Tony Blair or Margaret Thatcher doing this, and b) at what Harold Wilson would have done with the internet.

May 1979

The infamous 'Winter of Discontent' of 1978 – stories have abounded since of endless power cuts, rubbish piling up in the streets and people being unable to bury the dead. Prime minister Jim Callaghan flew back into Britain from a summit in Guadeloupe and declared that things were not as bad as the media were making out – which was immediately immortalised as the headline: 'Crisis? What Crisis?', one of those famous 'never-uttered' quotes which, nonetheless, has become one of the few things people are still able to recall about 'Sunny Jim'.* His refusal to go to the country in autumn 1978 – famously singing 'There was I, waiting at the church' at the party conference to rub it in – was beginning, by early 1979, to look like a bad call. And after losing a confidence motion by one vote on 28 March 1979, Callaghan was obliged to call the election – and his Labour party lost to Margaret Thatcher.

---

* Headline in the *Sun*, 11 January 1979.

Famous for being the bogeywoman 'milk snatcher' (as education secretary) to those of us who grew up in the 1970s, 'Maggie' was now the country's first ever female prime minister. At the door to Downing Street, surrounded by burly policemen and backed by cheers and jeers in equal measure, she quoted St Francis of Assisi: 'Where there is discord, may we bring harmony. Where there is error, may we bring truth. Where there is doubt, may we bring faith. And where there is despair, may we bring hope.'* A quick look back over the turbulent 1980s suggests that the debate as to whether or not she succeeded isn't likely to be over for a while yet.

June 1983

No leader of the twentieth century divides opinion quite like Margaret Hilda Thatcher. Nobody who grew up in the 1970s or 1980s is indifferent to her. Depending on who you ask – perhaps, more tellingly, *where* you ask – she was either:

a) the saviour of Britain, a resolute 'Iron Lady' who dragged the country up by its bootlaces out of a quagmire of strikes, economic disaster and industrial underperformance, and transformed it into an international powerhouse and major world player

or:

b) a heartless, monetarist harridan who is going to find her grave desecrated in various unmentionable ways when she finally shuffles off this mortal coil (and don't think she hasn't thought ahead about this one by arranging to be buried at sea); a bogeywoman who

---

* BBC News, 4 May 1979.

ripped the soul from the working heartlands of the country, leaving it bruised and bleeding and never to recover.

As ever in such matters, one suspects the truth lies somewhere in between.

In 1983, though, everything was going Mrs Thatcher's way. It hadn't looked so good for her just a couple of years before – with riots on the streets and unemployment queues growing, it looked very much as if this Tory administration could end up being a three-year wonder. But, as other leaders before and since have discovered, there's nothing like a good war for getting your ratings up. Bring on the Falklands Conflict of 1982, in which a British task force sailed forth to reclaim some unknown islands which most British people probably still couldn't find on a map. (My school's geography teacher at the time had the unenviable task that year of teaching the class about Argentina – obviously the international situation could not have been foreseen when planning the year's curriculum.) Almost overnight, it seemed, Maggie was transformed – poking her bescarfed head up out of tanks, telling us all to 'rejoice' and trouncing the increasingly desperate and unconvincing Labour leader Michael Foot in the House of Commons.

However, she was confronted on national TV by viewer Diana Gould in the Bristol studio, a woman who wouldn't let it lie – with, ironically, a Thatcher-like tenacity – about the sinking of the Argentine battleship *General Belgrano*.* Still, as Mrs Thatcher herself said at the time, in 2012 all the facts will be published, and we'll see who was right – so not long to wait now.

---

* BBC *Nationwide*, 24 May 1982.

In June 1983, Thatcher's Conservatives gained 37 extra seats – the last time to date that a sitting government has actually upped its majority.

Like its spiritual twin, the 1997 election, this fight was a kicking through and through – and one from which it seemed the loser would take the best part of a decade to recover. In fact, it seemed even the elements were ranged against Labour. When they were valiantly trying to relaunch themselves under new leader Neil Kinnock on Brighton beach, Neil fell over in front of the cameras and almost ended up in the sea – thus setting the agenda for the record nine years of frustration and failure which would dog him as opposition leader.

Yes, in 1983 the Tories seemed invincible. It looked as if they could never again lose an election. Card-carrying lefties sobbed into their beers and berets, wondering if they might as well give it all up now and start investing in offshore accounts. The Labour party was an irrelevance, about to tear itself apart and disappear, the Liberals were fumbling in the dark, the SDP were a joke and the Ecology party (later the Greens) were a bunch of comical peddlers of disaster.

A week is a long time in politics. Fourteen years, as we will see, may as well be in another temporal dimension altogether.

The most boring election? 1987. Because we knew we were going to lose for the third time and yet we'd come a long way since 1983. If we'd received a school report for our performance in 1987, it would have said, no doubt, 'progressing well, but could do better'.

Angela Smith MP

May 1997

Regardless of one's opinion on the result, the election of 1997 surely has to be seen as the most seismic shift in the British political landscape of the last 30 years. In case you need reminding, there was a Labour landslide, resulting in a record majority of 179 seats. After four terms, the Tories were finally defeated and the new, glossy, shiny PM, Tony Blair, was ushered in on a wave of sunshine, flags and cheering people in Downing Street (whom some cynics suspected of being Labour party members and not ordinary members of the public). Tony flashed heliograph messages with his teeth as he made his way (perhaps floating a little off the ground) up Downing Street. 'New! Better! Labour!' said the teeth, and a nation reeled in anticipation.

John Major had hung on as long as he possibly could, because even he knew that he was going to lose this one. He even managed to keep the same haircut and glasses for the whole five years. In 1995, he had been re-elected leader of the party with his famous 'put up or shut up' resignation as party leader – the vote of confidence in him, while enough to keep him in the post, was perhaps not as high as he'd have liked, but he was still widely seen as the only man able to unite a Tory party which was fatally split over the Europe issue. Now, he was off to watch the cricket and drink warm beer, leaving the Tories to their sorry mess.

The one man who could perhaps have defeated him, Michael Portillo – who had even got as far as installing phone lines in a campaign headquarters for the purpose – had bottled it at the last minute in 1995. His famous defeat at the 1997 election provided just one of many memorable moments, with Labour's Stephen Twigg rolling his eyes in a 'gosh, you mean me?' way as the vote was announced.

The entire country appeared bewitched and bamboozled by Blair, as if Labour had ordered not only the victory but also the weather, and Britain would now be a land of organic milk and honey where everybody was fair and nice and just. It only took a month or two for his 'yoof' appeal to wear off, when he appeared on the cover of the *NME* alongside the famous John Lydon quote: 'Ever get the feeling you've been cheated?' The rest of the country seemed to come round to this way of thinking eventually.

Blair, of course, is another of those politicians who divides public opinion in the way Thatcher does, although not so neatly down political divisions. So, he was either:

a) the saviour of Britain, a bold reformer who took centre-left policies and remoulded a country in dire need of change, ensuring continuity of approach and consistency of purpose, finding the fabled 'Third Way' between socialism and conservatism while taking difficult but necessary decisions

or:

b) a phoney car salesman in a sharp suit, who pushed through a right-wing agenda under the guise of Labour policies, a traitor to socialism who sacrificed everything for electability, an immaculate package with no substance and, furthermore, a warmonger at the beck and call of George W. Bush.

History, no doubt, will provide its verdict in due course. It's interesting, though, that Rayner and Stapley, in their book *Debunking History*, challenge the idea that Blair was some kind of traitor to socialism, arguing that the British Labour party was not as firmly rooted in a socialist agenda as is often thought.[*]

Everyone has their own favourite moment from the 1997 election. One could mention Jeremy Paxman asking Cecil Parkinson: 'You famously own a fertiliser company. Just how deep is the, er, *mess* that your party is in now?' The question was to be answered over the next decade with two more election defeats and three unsuccessful leaders in rapid succession. The Conservative party struggled to keep its head above the manure – and some said it was dead.

But times change. David Cameron's leadership is seen as a light at the end of the tunnel, especially in view of the party's best poll ratings in two decades. There are still rumblings about the sacrifices which have had to be made, not least the views of the Tory rank and file being brushed aside in Cameron's attempt to occupy the 'big tent' of the centre ground of British politics.

> *1992 was the most exciting because it was the closest, and the outcome wasn't known until the night of the election. 2001 was the dullest because everyone knew the result before the campaign started.*
>
> Iain Dale, blogger, with more election memories

* Ed Rayner and Ron Stapley, *Debunking History: 152 Popular Myths Exploded*: The History Press Ltd., 2006.

A dishonourable mention: June 2001

The most boring and predictable general election in living memory, dubbed the 'quiet landslide' by the press.

It was a historic milestone as it returned a Labour government for a second consecutive term – on a very safe manifesto, which may as well have read: 'We promise to give you all lots of money, be terribly nice and look clean at all times, not like that other lot.' Those looking for a 'Portillo moment' might have been temporarily excited by Blair aide Peter Mandelson's almost comically defiant speech on his re-election, in which he declared that he was 'a fighter and not a quitter'. But there were no great revelations or memorable moments as in 1997's landslide, and none of the tension, drama or edge-of-the-seat moments provided by the best elections of the 1970s and 1980s. Perhaps the most exciting event was the timetabling of the election, delayed by a month because of the foot-and-mouth outbreak.

There is a theory that turnout is high when people think a result is going to be close, and that it's low when it's seen as being in the bag for one party. With Labour predicted to win comfortably again, the 2001 election had, at 59.4 per cent, the lowest turnout of any post-war general election. (Only nine years earlier, at the hard-to-call 1992 election, 77.7 per cent of voters had made it to the ballot box.) And something must really have demotivated the good people of Liverpool Riverside in 2001, as only a measly 34 per cent of them were able to drag themselves to the polling station. Four always-keen Northern Irish constituencies featured at the top of the turnout tree, but in England it was the electorate of Norfolk North who managed the highest level of engagement, clocking up a healthy 75 per cent.

So what actually happened? Result after result came in, looking much the same as last time. Most people had probably gone to bed by midnight, waking up to see the not-unexpected news that William Hague had fallen on his sword early in the morning. Charles Kennedy and the Liberal Democrats did well, increasing their share of the vote and adding a net total of six seats.

Hague had, at the time, seemed quite promising – 'Tory Boy' image aside (see the cringeworthy speech from the 1979 Conservative party conference at which the sixteen-year-old William oleaginously displayed both his Thatcherite credentials and the worst haircut outside *Grange Hill*). He was young, fresh, pretty much unheard of (he'd been Welsh secretary before, hardly a stellar Cabinet role) and had a very photogenic girl-friend, Ffion, whom he later married. Somewhere along the line, though, Hague's image was mismanaged, result-ing in his appearance at the Notting Hill Carnival in a baseball cap and some very odd stories about his teenage drinking capacity.

The problem, in reality, was never Hague. In the early 1990s, John Major had, against the odds, held together a fragmenting Tory party which had never been as popu-lar as it was in the mid-eighties, and somehow he had squeezed out an unexpected fourth victory in 1992. But now, here was a Conservative party which had run out of steam, and which was still bruised and battered from the 1997 defeat. Hague frequently got the better of Tony Blair in debate, and most weeks in the Commons man-aged to be witty while doing so, but it did not do him much good. That the party would return to power so soon after such a good kicking in 1997 was a delusion which, one suspects, even the most diehard true-blue struggled to believe.

For Hague, resigning turned out to be the best thing he ever did – he has since remained in Parliament, forging a side-career out of public speaking and writing and emerging as a statesmanlike and dignified shadow foreign secretary, and is still one of the best debaters there are. Those in the know say he's quite happy where he is and doesn't fancy another tilt at the leadership – so for now, he keeps his place in history as one of the few Conservative leaders to leave office without having been prime minister. That list also includes Sir Joseph Austen Chamberlain and Michael 'something of the night' Howard. It also includes Iain 'the quiet man' Duncan Smith, ousted after just two years in the role and never even having a go at a general election. Commentators who wanted to portray Duncan Smith as the party's version of a reforming Kinnock-type figure were laughed at because deep down, everybody knew the real comparison – IDS was the Tories' Michael Foot.

Ultimately, about the most exciting thing one can say on the subject of the 2001 election is that around 100 more votes nationally were cast for the New Millennium Bean Party than for the Workers' Revolutionary Party, which was probably a sign of the times.

Which seat holds the record for the quickest result?

Polling booths close at 10.00pm, and very few seats manage to declare a result before midnight. The voters of Sunderland South, for three successive general elections, have basked in the glory of being in the first constituency to declare. Labour's Chris Mullin retained the seat in 2005, albeit with a slightly reduced majority. In 1997, it took just 46 minutes to produce a result. In 2001, the result was declared at 10.43pm, and in 2005 it was declared just 45 seconds later, meaning that the 2001 record stands.

Now that the authorities of Sunderland South have realised the media attention which the record brings them, they actively try to break it at every election – by employing extra vote-counters, plus the rather danger-ous-sounding practice of manipulating the town's traffic lights to allow the vans carrying the ballot boxes through as quickly as possible. However, Sunderland can be rather less proud of the fact that plummeting voter turnout has also added to the ease of the count.

TV election expert Peter Snow has pointed out that the result is a good early indicator for the BBC – as a safe Labour seat it gives them some idea of the extent of the swing. It's always fun to claim to know what's happening in advance. Talking of which ...

Political crystal balls

Psephologists, the people who study voting and election form, love informed speculation – and a lot of the time that's all they have to keep them going until the next round of elections comes along. It's a game you can play at home. And it's all the more entertaining when the experts are revealed to be off-beam.

Bush vs. Kerry, 2004: In a close contest between two can-didates, there are inevitably going to be some premature calls, but things seem to have gone spectacularly wrong for some of the few pundits who dared predict the outcome of the 2004 US presidential election. Slate.com, the US online magazine of news, politics and culture, had Democrat John Kerry leading the race over George W. Bush by ten electoral votes as late as 31 October. The Fox News channel decided to stop using the exit poll results, denouncing them as unreliable, when the real numbers coming in started to show that the early predictions for John Kerry were over-inflated. In the UK, Labour spin doctor Alastair Campbell called the predictions a 'mug's game' although, undeterred, MORI founder and chairman Robert Worcester confidently called the election for John Kerry live on ITV! Most experts played it safe by confining themselves to the 'prediction' that the race would be one of the closest in living memory. **Crystal balls: ✪✪**

Kinnock vs. Major, 1992: The one where even the exit polls got it wrong in the UK, although nobody doubted the closeness of the fight. The Tories, against the odds, scraped back in with a majority of 21. In the end, Labour leader Neil Kinnock's prematurely triumphant 1992 Sheffield rally speech, which he later described as being brought about by a 'rush of blood', was seen to have been a great part of his undoing – although some cite lingering suspicion of his support for unilateral nuclear disarmament as a problem, even though he threw out that policy in 1987. 'This roar hit me,' Kinnock said of the 1992 rally, 'and for a couple of seconds I responded to it; and all of the years in which I'd attempted to build a fairly reserved, starchy persona – in a few seconds they slipped away.'* **Crystal balls: ✪**

* Quoted by Michael Leapman in the *Independent*, 26 November 1995.

Tips for the Top, 2004: Party grandees Steve Norris of the Conservatives, Neil Kinnock of Labour and Baroness Williams of the Liberal Democrats were all collared by the BBC in 2004 and asked to pick out the 'rising stars' of their respective parties. Norris appears to have scored the biggest hits, citing the then little-known David Cameron, George Osborne and Chris Grayling as Tory fast-trackers, although Kinnock didn't do badly either by spotting future Cabinet stars David Miliband, Douglas Alexander and Yvette Cooper. Meanwhile, Shirley Williams pointed accurately to Ed Davey as a rising Lib Dem, plus Vincent Cable and Simon Hughes as established names who would continue to give the party stability. Not a bad assessment all round. **Crystal balls: ✪✪✪✪✪**

Guardian/**ICM polls, 1997–2005:** One thing we hear a lot, usually from the party which is currently doing badly, is that 'the only poll which matters is the one on election day' – and it's fair to say that the spectre of 1992, when the pollsters got it so wrong, still hangs over any predictions. But the polls by research company ICM for the *Guardian* newspaper have proved to be surprisingly accurate – a selection of phone polls from two years before each of the last elections shows that they got the winner right and the margin to within 2–4 per cent in 1997 and 2005, and the right result (although with, it's fair to say, a worse result predicted for the Conservatives than they actually got) in 2001.* **Crystal balls: ✪✪✪✪**

---

* ICM/*Guardian* polls at http://www.icmresearch.co.uk/media-centre-voting-intentions.php

PolFax: Worst of a Bad Bunch?

In Channel 4's somewhat mean-spirited 2005 poll of '100 Worst Britons', several were politicians – Tony Blair and Margaret Thatcher ranked the highest, with 'disgraced Tory MP' Neil Hamilton (and his wife Christine) coming in at number nineteen and Edwina Currie at number 26. For Labour, Ken Livingstone and John Prescott appeared at numbers 50 and 87 respectively. Peter Tatchell was there at 80, while Iain Duncan Smith and Ann Widdecombe kept the Tory end up in the lower reaches. Here is the Top Ten, showing the esteemed company our two former PMs kept:

1. Tony Blair: prime minister at the time, never a popular job
2. Jordan: aka Katie Price, pneumatic and ubiquitous 'reality TV' star and model
3. Margaret Thatcher: former 'Iron Lady' and PM
4. Jade Goody: another 'reality' star
5. Martin Bashir: TV reporter famous for interviewing Princess Diana and Michael Jackson
6. Gareth Gates: singer of innocuous pop songs
7. Alex Ferguson: hot-tempered football manager
8. 'H' from Steps: campest member of a camp singing fivesome
9. Geri Halliwell: red-haired former Spice Girl
10. HM Queen Elizabeth II: tenacious monarch

PolFax: The Essentials of the Most Recent Prime Ministers

Name: Harold Wilson
Party: Labour
First MP: 1945
First party leader: 1963
First PM: 1964
Age when became PM: 48
In power: 1964–70, 1974–76

Elections won: 4 (1964, 1966, February 1974, October 1974)
Elections lost: 1 (1970)
Manner of removal: Stepped down as leader in 1976

Nickname: Doesn't appear to have had one, but the 'Lavender List' was the nickname given to his resignation honours list in 1976
Style: Pipe-smoking 'man of the people'
Infamy: Various conspiracy theories abound about threats to 'remove' Wilson from power in the 1960s

Low point: Leaving office with his reputation damaged after the economic problems of his 1970s premiership
High point: 1963 party conference speech referring to the 'white heat' of technology
History will remember as: Most successful Labour PM until Blair came along

Name: Edward Heath
Party: Conservative
First MP: 1950
First party leader: 1965
First PM: 1970
Age when became PM: 53
In power: 1970–74

Elections won: 1 (1970)
Elections lost: 3 (1966, February 1974 and October 1974)
Manner of removal: Resigned as prime minister after coalition talks failed following the hung parliament of February 1974. Lost party leadership contest in 1975 after losing the October 1974 election

Nickname: The Grocer (thanks to his negotiations with the Common Market over food prices while Harold Macmillan's minister of labour)
Style: Curmudgeonly and no-nonsense
Infamy: The famous '30-year sulk' which marked his frosty relationship with Mrs Thatcher

Low point: Coming to be seen as a liability for the party after losing three out of four general elections
High point: 1975's referendum campaign in which Britain voted to remain in the EEC
History will remember as: Governing during a turbulent period – the 'three-day week' and confrontation with the unions, as well as the bloodiest time in the Northern Ireland Troubles

Name: James Callaghan
Party: Labour
First MP: 1945
First party leader: 1976
First PM: 1976
Age when became PM: 64
In power: 1976–79

Elections won: 0
Elections lost: 1 (1979)
Manner of removal: Lost 1979 election and resigned as leader

Nickname: Sunny Jim
Style: Your friendly local high-street bank manager
Infamy: His 'Crisis? What crisis?' moment during the Winter of Discontent

Low point: Struggling in government during the strikes of 1978
High point: So far the only person to have been home secretary, foreign secretary, chancellor and prime minister
History will remember as: Putting a brave face on a difficult time of industrial unrest

Name: Margaret Thatcher
Party: Conservative
First MP: 1959
First party leader: 1975
First PM: 1979
Age when became PM: 53
In power: 1979–90

Elections won: 3 (1979, 1983, 1987)
Elections lost: 0
Manner of removal: Stabbed in the back by own party

Nickname: The Iron Lady, The Grocer's Daughter
Style: Hectoring, patronising, with total or self-belief
Infamy: Unemployment, riots, the poll tax – hated throughout vast areas of the country for apparent lack of concern for the unemployed and unfortunate

Low point: Leaving Downing Street when she knew it was all over
High point: Creating homeowners by allowing purchase of council houses; restoration of Britain to status of major European and world player
History will remember as: a divisive figure, and the UK's first female PM

Name: John Major
Party: Conservative
First MP: 1979
First party leader: 1990
First PM: 1990
Age when became PM: 47
In power: 1990–96

Elections won: 1 (1992)
Elections lost: 1 (1997)
Manner of removal: Lost the 1997 election, resigned as leader hours later

Nickname: The Grey Man, Honest John
Style: Diffident, 'man of the people', cricket-loving

Infamy: Having his 'Back to Basics' campaign undermined by various ministers' sexual shenanigans

Low point: Continually undermined as leader and gradually saw his majority eroded during the Parliament of 1992–97

High point: Continually striving for peace in Northern Ireland, a process which eventually led to the Good Friday Agreement of 1998

History will remember as: An essentially decent man who struggled to hold together a fragmenting party

Name: Tony Blair
Party: Labour
First MP: 1983
First party leader: 1994
First PM: 1997
Age when became PM: 43
In power: 1997–2007

Elections won: 3 (1997, 2001, 2005)
Elections lost: 0
Manner of removal: Quit before being pushed

Nickname: Phoney Tony, Teflon Tony
Style: Superficial sincerity, offset with humour and 'spin'
Infamy: Student tuition fees, the Iraq War

Low point: Seeing his initial popularity plummet after getting close to George W. Bush and supporting military action in Iraq

High point: Free admission to museums and galleries in UK; introduction of civil partnerships

History will remember as: George's grinning buddy in Iraq, sadly

Name: Gordon Brown
Party: Labour
First MP: 1983
First party leader: 2007
First PM: 2007
Age when became PM: 56
In power: 2007–10 (and history will judge how much longer)

Elections won: 0, probably
Elections lost: 1, probably
Manner of removal: Very probably losing the 2010 election

Nickname: The Clunking Fist, Bottler Brown
Style: Straightforward, dour, easily rattled
Infamy: Claiming to have 'saved the world' while the economy collapsed around him; seeing his reputation as a 'prudent' chancellor undermined by the credit crunch and global downturn

Low point: The continuing challenges to his authority throughout his time in power, and the persistent press rumours about a 'coup' of some form
High point: His time as chancellor – until the recession made his 'no return to boom and bust' catchphrase something of a joke
History will remember as: The recession PM

The Numbers Game: Terrible Twos

2: General elections held in 1974

2: General elections won by Harold Wilson in 1974

2: MPs called 'Angela Smith' in the 2005–10 Parliament

2: Majority initially won by MP Mark Oaten in Winchester in 1992

2: Candidates fielded by the Socialist party in 1950

2: Times David Davis stood for the Tory leadership

2: Percentage of people who rated 'poverty/inequality' as the most important issue facing Britain today in the July 2008 Ipsos-MORI Issues Index Survey

2: Percentage of people who rated 'morality' as the most important issue facing Britain today in the same survey (The top single issue was 'Economy' with 18 per cent)

2: Resignations by Peter Mandelson from Tony Blair's Cabinet

Vox Pops

Just think it through from my perspective. You are the prime minister, with a majority of eighteen, a party that is still harking back to a golden age that never was, and is now invented. You have three rightwing members of the Cabinet who actually resign. What happens in the parliamentary party?

John Major, prime minister 1990–97, on those in his Cabinet who, shall we say, weren't entirely behind him. Or if they were, only stood there to wield a knife.

4

Honourable Members: Rules, regulations and ribaldry

When I left the dining room after sitting next to Mr Gladstone,
I thought he was the cleverest man in England. But after
sitting next to Mr Disraeli, I thought I was the cleverest
woman in England.
Attributed to various, including Queen Victoria
and Jennie Jerome

Becoming an MP

Inevitably, as you become more interested in politics, the thought will occur to you at some point that 'I could do that'. For most people, it is never much more than an idle boast, perhaps even a joke. But what if you decide you would genuinely like to do the job?

- Unless you're a high-profile character 'parachuted' into a safe seat – which, to be honest, happens rarely – becoming an MP is a long, hard road involving a lot of footwork and handshaking. Most MPs are people who have been active in local politics, serving their time as party members and activists and helping others to get elected. They may well have been expected to fight unwinnable seats first.

- You will almost certainly need some party affiliation. In 70 years, only eleven independent MPs have been elected to the UK Parliament – so it's not impossible, but difficult. You need to be over the age of eighteen (it was 21 until recently), and not be a peer in the House of Lords, a bishop, an undischarged bankrupt, a judge, a civil servant, a member of the armed forces, a police officer or a prisoner.

- You will also need a deposit of £500, which you'll lose if you fail to gain 5 per cent of the overall vote. And it does happen, even to the major parties – Labour's candidate in the 2008 Henley by-election lost his, for example, gaining fewer votes than the Greens and the far-right British National Party, and while it's fair to say that leafy, affluent Henley was never a seat Labour expected to win, that result was seen as pretty disastrous.

- Your permitted expenses will be £100,000, and be careful not to fiddle them – in 1999, Labour's Fiona Jones became the first MP in 140 years to lose a seat as a result of falsifying election expenses. Unless you have been living in a cave or on Mars for the past couple of years, you will have noticed that this issue has become a major political hot potato. It seemed that the extent of the 'creative' use of expenses was never-ending – grocery bills, duck houses, pornographic DVDs and even receipts for small everyday items came under scrutiny as public outrage grew. Even MPs who had previously been considered 'decent' and would ordinarily have been given a fair hearing by most people, like Sir Menzies Campbell, started to receive hostile receptions in public as the news of ostentatious refurbishments filtered through. It's fair to say that the expenses scandal shook up the House of Commons in a major way, and while the regulations

continue to be finalised, public trust in MPs is only
slowly being rebuilt. This, of course, doesn't help the
aspiring MP to feel more confident – or does it? One
could argue that the current climate favours new
faces over incumbents, with the public mood being
very much in favour of a fresh face. Time will tell.

- Those who have been there and done it variously rec-
ommend other strategies and tips such as: not losing
sight of why you are trying to become an MP in the
first place, persevering, developing a thick skin, having a trusted circle of colleagues, being grateful for
any party support you can get and being expected to
do a lot of the work yourself.

- The Electoral Commission website at www.electoral-
commission.org.uk has everything else you'll need to
know, including downloadable documents for candidates and agents, who manage a candidate's campaign in their constituency – as well as information
on registering to vote and being an electoral observer.

Your MP

If you don't know who your MP is – *find out*. It's incredibly easy to do so and the chances are that, at some point,
you'll need to know. Go to www.aboutmyvote.co.uk and
enter your postcode – it'll give you details of your city
council as well as your local MP, their party affiliation and
contact details. Or go to the online listing of MPs' contact details at the UK Parliament website to find out their
email and web address.[*]

---

[*] See http://www.parliament.uk/directories/hciolists/alms.cfm

What can and can't your MP do?

Your MP is there to represent local constituents. That's you, whether you voted for him/her or not. They make and scrutinise legislation, attend various debates and committees, and are generally there to protect, to advocate and to promote the interests of their constituency at a national level.

Things they can't do include:

- Getting preferential treatment for you, no matter how much of an injustice you feel has been served

- Helping with private disputes between you and other individuals

- Interfering in decisions which have been made by the courts

- It also isn't always appropriate for them to interfere in decisions which have been made by the local council, where it may be more appropriate to contact the relevant council service, followed by a local councillor

- Offering legal advice. If you ask for it, their office will probably redirect you to the Citizens' Advice Bureau

- On an immigration or asylum issue, they can only write to the Home Office on your behalf if there has been an inappropriate delay in dealing with the case

- In the House of Commons, they can't accuse another MP of lying, suggest another MP has false motives, misrepresent another MP's words or use 'abusive or insulting language'. If an MP uses 'unparliamentary' language, the Speaker will ask them to withdraw it

And remember:
- There is a strict Parliamentary rule that an MP can only look after and take up the cases of people who live in his/her own constituency.

Always ask: where does the buck stop and how can I get rid of them? That's my fundamental view of what democracy is all about.

Gisela Stuart MP

MPs are asked to take an Oath of Allegiance to the Queen, which is as follows: 'I swear by Almighty God that I will be faithful and bear true allegiance to Her Majesty Queen Elizabeth, her heirs and successors, according to law. So help me God.' There is now a non-religious variant, in which members 'solemnly, sincerely and truly declare and affirm' their allegiance. Some MPs push their luck as far as they can with it – the late Tony Banks was one who recited the oath with his fingers crossed.

In April 2008, the Republic campaign group published a suggested letter to Justice Secretary Jack Straw on their website, in which they asked for an alternative oath for those with republican sensibilities to be considered. And more recently there has been a move, backed by 22 MPs, to have the oath to the Queen removed by an oath of allegiance to constituents. This didn't go down well with Tory grandee Lord Tebbit, who fulminated:

If something has worked satisfactorily for the past 500 years, as the oath of allegiance has, the fact that a silly group of people at the beginning of the twenty-first century think they know better seems to me to be a very dodgy proposition.[*]

Communication

Your MP is supposed to send you a polite response to your queries, although sometimes – amusingly – some interpret this in their own way. In 2008, Tyne Bridge MP David Clelland, in response to a constituent who wrote him a concerned letter about civil liberties, decided it would be a good idea to say:

> I accept your offer not to vote for me again … I do not want your vote so you can stick it wherever best pleases you.[†]

This sort of behaviour is generally viewed with great disapproval. If you want to be re-elected, it's accepted that you smile, you shake hands and you are generally nice to people. Even those who accuse you of propping up a corrupt government, or call you a totalitarian, venal weasel. It's in the nature of the job.

In 1996, MP Michael Stern, who at the time represented Bristol North West, branded one of his constituents the 'neighbour from hell', saying: 'I have received reports of threats against other children; of fighting in the house, the garden and the street outside; of people coming and going 24 hours a day – in particular a series of men late at night – of rubbish and stolen cars dumped nearby; of glass strewn in the road; of alleged

---

[*] Quoted by James Chapman in the *Daily Mail*, 8 August 2008.
[†] Reported by Will Pavia in *The Times*, 2 July 2008.

drug activity.'* It's a fair assumption that he didn't follow that up with a doorstep visit to say: 'I trust I can count on your vote?'

In 2007, an assistant to Stockton MP Dari Taylor put his foot in it when his accompanying note to Ms Taylor in a forwarded email about a constituent was sent back to the constituent instead. The offending message said: 'I have spoken to her mother about the issue at length and she's very snotty. Hates the government and wasn't afraid to say so. So no rush.'†

Sometimes, MPs communicate unwisely within their own parties. Examples are numerous, but one rebel Labour MP who spoke out against her leader in 2008 must have rued the day she wrote 'Gordon Brown would be a disaster' on the nomination papers in the party leadership election. The papers were numbered, and therefore she could be identified. Something else to look out for if you ever go into politics.

Ministers for Fitness

It has been said, rather cruelly, that politics is 'showbiz for ugly people'. Quite why people's looks should be a factor in their ability to do the job is a mystery, but MPs are, to some extent, subject to the same media scrutiny as other 'famous' people.

In October 2007, Home Secretary Jacqui Smith told journalists obsessed with her cleavage to 'get over themselves', saying: 'Honestly, the morning when I made the statement to the House about the terror incidents that

---

* Quoted by Sean O'Neill in 'MP names "neighbour from hell"', *Daily Telegraph*, 18 July 1996.
† 'MP refuses to apologise to constituent branded snotty', *Northern Echo*, 15 March 2007.

I had faced on my first weekend ... funnily enough the main thing on my mind when I got up was not: "Is my top too low cut or not?""* In December 2007, Quentin Letts – also a fan, it should be noted in passing, of Jacqui's cleavage – waxed lyrical in the *Daily Mail* about Transport Secretary Ruth Kelly's transformation into a 'blonde-tressed lovely', citing her 'souped-up wardrobe' and 'radiantly fuchsia jacket'.†

The same organ fawned over 'Sarkozy's Sirens', devoting a double-page spread to the lavish ball gowns of some of the new set of French ministers as they arrived at an official dinner. Justice Minister Rachida Dati 'wore a stunning floor-length blue gown slashed nearly to the thigh', while minister of culture Christine Albanel managed to look 'dignified and stateswoman-like' in her 'black taffeta, sleek hair and understated make-up', apparently. Various unflattering comparisons were made with the 'Dowdy Street' fashions of Hazel Blears, Harriet Harman and Ruth Kelly. Oh, and all of this came from a female journalist.‡ It is fair to say that a male politician of similar stature would not have been subjected to the same kind of extraordinary comment.

We haven't yet got to the stage of voting for them in *X Factor*-style polls, but maybe it's only a matter of time. In the meantime, the media console themselves with superficial commentary on the physical appearance of our Honourable Members. With such 'froth' dominating the agenda, can we really blame the voters if they are underinformed about the substance?

---

* Quoted by Andy McSmith in 'Jacqui Smith: Mrs Sensible', *Independent*, 7 June 2008.
† Quentin Letts, 'From ugly duckling to swan: What's transformed Ruth Kelly?' *Daily Mail*, 19 December 2007.
‡ Liz Jones, 'Sarkozy's Sirens', *Daily Mail*, 12 March 2008.

A more light-hearted example is the *Daily Mail*'s Sexiest MPs Poll, published each year on Valentine's Day.* It would, of course, demonstrate an unhealthy obsession with superficial trivia to discuss the results here. So let's only do so briefly. Conservative Jeremy Hunt topped the 2008 list but proved to be surprisingly reticent on the subject of his win. He has since caused ructions by posting some thoughts on graffiti on his blog, saying that, no matter how objectionable the principle, some 'can be very thought-provoking'. Also feted were the Bromsgrove Tory MP Julie Kirkbride, a perennial fixture in these polls of pulchritudinous politicians, and the Lib Dems' telegenic Julia Goldsworthy, tipped by some as a future leader of her party. The oldest entry in the list, at 56, was Lynne Featherstone (Lib Dem, Hornsey and Wood Green). Her comment on the list was that it is 'a self-identified bit of fun for a moment' and one which is not sexist as it 'picks on both men and women'. Lib Dem leader Nick Clegg got a mention, which resulted in Tory MP Ed Vaizey commenting: 'Nick's a lovely guy but he's terribly vain. For the entire trip [their joint Arctic trek in October 2007] he harped on about how he was number one in a Sky poll of "Most Fanciable MPs" and that I was only number nine. We shared an igloo and the intimate, bonding evening chat was based on how good-looking he is. I was referred to only by my fanciability ranking of number nine.'† Perhaps also disappointed was housing minister Caroline Flint, runner-up in 2007 and spectacularly plummeting out of the Top Ten in 2008 – although perhaps she can take comfort from being the winner of the 'Sexiest Female MP' award in Julian Worricker's

* Sky News, 14 February 2008.
† Quoted in *New Statesman*, 18 October 2007.

Political Awards on BBC Radio 5 Live. Conservative Nadine Dorries also lost out this time round despite having a big following.

As for the rest of the world, we are reliably informed of the large fan base of Marianne Thieme, photogenic face of the Netherlands' Party For The Animals, who have two seats in the Dutch parliament. She was, perhaps ambiguously, voted 'Political Talent of the Year' in 2006. Women's magazine *Viva* gave her the title of 'Most Spicy Politician of the Netherlands'. Bill Clinton's saxophone-playing charisma still works on ladies of a certain age – coupled, perhaps, with a nostalgia for simpler times which manifests itself as a fondness for the days of Bill. And new incumbent Barack Obama has his fans, as does his erstwhile rival (and possible future nemesis) Sarah Palin, the Republicans' gun-toting, elk-slaying, take-no-prisoners rising star. Palin's interview with ABC News's Charlie Gibson betrayed a worrying lack of foreign policy experience.* Unlike her namesake Michael, she hadn't exactly been *Pole To Pole* – she freely admitted to only ever having visited Canada, Mexico and (briefly) Kuwait, and seemed to think that the fact that her neighbours could see Russia from their front doors gave them huge insights into Vladimir Putin's policies.

It should be noted that people can get into trouble for this sort of thing. In 2007 the *Guardian* reported that a discussion on the relative merits of female Labour MPs had been left running on David Cameron's webcameron.org.uk site before anybody thought to get rid of it. Labour's Caroline Flint – yes, her again, amusingly, the minister for fitness at the time – said:

---

* Reported by Jill Zuckman in the *Chicago Tribune*, 12 September 2008.

If this puerile nonsense is what passes for debate in the Cameron Tory party, they have a long way to go. Only today have they finally become too embarrassed to let this schoolboy tripe remain on their website.[*]

However, this didn't stop her posing seductively in a national newspaper wearing a slinky red designer dress following her resignation from Gordon Brown's Cabinet in June 2009.

All of this may lead to sympathy for ministers who accuse the media of being more interested in 'froth' and 'fluff' than in the substance of their policies. But perhaps this kind of coverage is a symptom, rather than a cause, of a malaise – the perception (wrong, of course) that 'they are all the same' and so it isn't 'worth talking about' policy issues, coupled with the assumption that people will find discussion of serious issues to be boring and that politics needs to be 'sexed-up'.

The 'baseball cap moment' and how to avoid it

We are in an age where politicians' every gesture, nuance and even change of attire is subjected to detailed semiotic scrutiny. David Cameron has become the first Conservative leader who sometimes undertakes official visits without a tie – it may sound a small thing, but even on a subconscious level, it sends out interesting signals from the leader of the party which is still often seen as the most 'stuffy' and old-fashioned. In fact, Cameron's adoption of the open-necked shirt is merely reflecting a growing trend – even in some quarters of the business

---

[*] Quoted by Rachel Williams in 'Tories remove web forum on MPs' looks', *Guardian*, 17 May 2007.

world, the tie is rapidly coming to be seen as a redundant item.

William Hague, as Conservative leader, was ridiculed in the press for sporting a baseball cap – not so much for the item itself (it makes sense for a gentleman who is losing his hair to cover up, after all) as for what it supposedly represented – an attempt to get in touch with 'yoof' culture. It seemed to undermine Hague as a politician, but in recent years he has re-emerged as a much more statesmanlike figure. In addition, the baseball cap is, a few years on, not really such a fashion faux pas after all – plenty of middle-aged men wear them in casual situations. Imagine the outcry if he had chosen to wear a hoodie.

Tony Blair, a masterful social chameleon, could often be seen relaxing both his body language and his speech mannerisms when in the company of people he thought would find him more amenable if he did so, such as sixth-formers. It sounded painful at times, especially his adoption of the Estuary glottal stop. Mrs Thatcher, less than a decade earlier, would never have done that – the grocer's daughter spoke to everyone, Queen or pauper, in the same rounded and slightly patronising tones.

Clothes, headgear, speech, gestures, off-the-cuff comments – they are all there to be analysed, pored over and viewed endlessly out of context on YouTube. It's difficult to see any way back. Politicians have always got it wrong in public, but these days, with 24-hour detailed scrutiny available, there is no way for them to pretend they got it right when they didn't.

'Gemma's got you by the ballots': politics and popular appeal

Another populist strand: the public seem to love 'maverick' politicians, perhaps because they mistrust the party system and respect anybody who can do well outside it. This affection doesn't often manifest itself as solid votes, but a few recent examples are interesting to note.

Vincent Cable's brief tenure as acting leader of the Lib Dems made him enormously popular, not least because he seemed to be enjoying it – and his place in British political anthologies is forever guaranteed thanks to his famous jibe to Gordon Brown: 'The house has noticed the prime minister's remarkable transformation in the past few weeks – from Stalin to Mr Bean.'* The crusading anti-sleaze MP Martin Bell won enormous affection for his iconic confrontation with disgraced Conservative Neil Hamilton in the fight for the Tatton constituency in 1997. And Miss Great Britain Gemma Garrett provided the nation with amusement – not to mention some entertaining tabloid headlines – when she chose to stand against David Davis in the high-profile Haltemprice and Howden by-election of 2008, promising the former shadow home secretary an 'elegantly bloody nose'.†

So is it possible to be a politician who people actually *like* a lot of the time? We are told that Sarah Palin's approval ratings as governor of Alaska were in the 90s, so she must have been doing something right. The problem, of course, comes when politicians have to stop talking and smiling and start acting – and we don't mean in the Ronald Reagan sense. Sooner or later, they have to

---

* *Hansard*, 28 November 2007: Column 275.
† Quoted by Bob Roberts in the *Daily Mirror*, 14 June 2008.

have some policies. And, personality cults aside, policies are what make you or break MPs.

Here are a few of those ideas which someone thought seemed like a good idea at the time, but which have bombed in recent years.

Twenty ways to win the voters over ... or not

1. Keep the Pound (2001)

At the 2001 general election, the Conservative leader William Hague campaigned to 'Keep The Pound', gambling that this would bring out the jingoistic Little Englander in the average voter – but it didn't work, despite vibrant Union Flag-themed placards and a gamble on the deeply Europhobic nature of the British people. They haven't tried it since. The question of whether or not to join the Euro is still a vexed one which successive governments have tried to ignore, but as the economic crisis brings the pound and the euro ever closer together, could it be on the cards? **Verdict: Not a sterling effort.**

2. Vote Paris! (2008)

John McCain's unsuccessful presidential campaign, concerned at the growing 'celebrity' status of Barack Obama, produced a video attempting to spin the Democrat's stardom as superficial, interspersing footage of him with videos of Paris Hilton and that other well-known political heavyweight, Britney Spears. But Paris hit back with her own broadcast. Referring to 'that wrinkly white-haired guy using me in his campaign ad', the intellectual hard-hitter faced the nation, reclining on a sun lounger in a leopard-skin-print swimsuit. She wanted America to know, she said, that she was 'like, totally ready to lead'.

Mentioning policies such as 'limited offshore drilling with strict environmental oversight' may, worryingly, have got some people believing that she was entirely serious, but her radical policies – pop star Rihanna for vice-president and painting the White House pink – may just have introduced the United States to the concept of irony. 'I hope that's cool with you guys,' she said as she signed off. **Verdict: Like, totally, Paris. See you in 2012 as Sarah's running-mate, honey.**

3. Handcuff pregnant prisoners (1997)

The Tories' highest-ranking woman since Mrs Thatcher was the fearsome Ann Widdecombe, member of the Conservative Christian Fellowship, novelist and vocal supporter of family values. She will forever be associated with two reported remarks – that she found 'something of the night' about her colleague Michael Howard, and that she allegedly didn't see anything wrong with handcuffing pregnant prisoners in transit. The former is a matter of record, but the latter is, shall we say, a little harder to pin down. The key phrase she used is that 'special treatment for pregnant prisoners could be abused', which some commentators were keen to spin as 'MAD WIDDY CHAINS UP MUMS IN PRISON'. **Verdict: Draconian.**

4. March hoodlums to the nearest cashpoint (2000)

In what he perhaps thought would be a popular move, Tony Blair announced in 2000 that on-the-spot fines should be given to violent drunks – which immediately raised the question of how the police officer should proceed if the offender had pissed all their wages up the wall and didn't happen to have any cash on them. It didn't help that, only a few days later, the prime minister's son

Euan, then aged sixteen, was apprehended for being drunk and incapable in Leicester Square. The policy was taken off the agenda more quickly than a rancid barrel being disconnected from the tap. **Verdict: ASBO.**

5. Ban drunken thugs from driving (2000)

And on a similar theme, here's another one Tony was working through in the middle of his first term – confiscate the driving licences of inebriated hoodlums and ban them from entering pubs. All very macho and 'tough on crime' in theory, but immediately dismissed by the police and the AA as unworkable – they knew many offenders would continue to drive anyway, that the removal of a driving licence would have knock-on effects on employment, and that there would have to be a correspondingly harsh punishment for non-drivers. **Verdict: Without due care and consideration.**

6. Call the food police (2000–01)

In an extraordinary Big Brother-style move, the government was supposedly considering having receipts monitored at the supermarket checkout to see if healthy eating policies were being pursued. Right? Well, again, this was something of a media exaggeration, based on the fact that the University of Leeds did some research, published in 2001, to see if till receipts could be used as a simple way of monitoring people's fat and energy intake. But you can just see this working, can't you? 'Mrs Wilkins, I see you've bought your Jimmy three bottles of blue pop, a pack of Minstrels and some Mother's Pride. Sounds all right to me.' Back to the drawing board with that one. **Verdict: Had its chips (and see also number 16).**

7. Bring in the poll tax (1990)

The poll tax replaced the rates (whose abolition had been promised in the Tories' 1979 manifesto) and was officially known as the 'Community Charge'. However, its medieval nickname had caught on so much that, in a debate, even Mrs Thatcher herself almost found herself using the phrase – to delighted jeers from the opposition benches. It was hugely unpopular as it appeared to shift the tax burden to the poor, was based on occupancy rather than house value and varied hugely from one council to the next. Demonstrations against the poll tax soon became riots, the best known of which occurred in London in 31 March 1990 and has been nicknamed the 'Battle of Trafalgar'. It was the biggest civil disturbance the capital had seen in the twentieth century. A hundred and thirteen people were injured and there were 340 arrests. John Major, in his first speech as PM, announced that the charge was to be scrapped and replaced with the council tax – which, while it cannot exactly be said to be popular, endures to this day. **Verdict: Riotous.**

8. Write the 'longest suicide note in history' (1983)

The Labour party manifesto of 1983, with its 'radical, socialist policies for reviving the British economy' (including unilateral disarmament and leaving the EEC) was labelled by Labour politician Gerald Kaufman as 'the longest suicide note in history', a nickname which has stuck. See if you agree by having a look at the online version.[*] **Verdict: Election-losing.**

---

[*] Labour Party Manifesto 1983. http://www.labour-party.org.uk/manifestos/1983

9. Go to war (1914–present day, on and off)

As Edwin Starr once said: 'War – what is it good for?' Margaret Thatcher's poll ratings shot up when she sent a task force to reclaim the Falkland Islands, and subsequently instructed the nation to 'rejoice'. On the other hand, the nation's patriotism was sorely tested when Tony Blair sent British troops to join the US forces in Iraq in 2003, in what many saw as an illegal war. **Verdict: Bellicose.**

10. Jail all asylum seekers (abolished 2008)

The Australian government abandoned this unpopular policy in 2008, with Amnesty International welcoming the fact that Australia had now come 'into line with other Western democracies'. It remains to be seen how long it takes before someone seriously suggests it in the UK. **Verdict:** *Daily Mail.*

11. Insult and abuse your opponents (2008)

Voters may think politicians spit and snarl at each other, but elections are more often than not carried out in a spirit of sporting rivalry. However, the prospective Tory party candidate for Watford had to step down after admitting to criminal damage and harassment, all aimed at his political opponents – his activities included tyre-slashing, silent phone calls, abusive graffiti and insulting letters. **Verdict: Inadvisable.**

12. Say 'there is no such thing as society' (1987)

An old chestnut. Margaret Thatcher, interviewed by *Woman's Own* in 1987, uttered the words 'there's no such thing as society', always quoted out of context and almost always brought up by her opponents years later. It's worth reading the whole thing to see just how wrong people get this when they quote it.* **Verdict: Lazily attributed.**

13. Try to 'bury bad news' (2001)

Oh, dear. Former government adviser Jo Moore is famous for one thing, namely saying on the day of the 11 September terror attacks that it might be a good day to 'bury' some controversial announcements. The exact wording of the memo is disputed, but it cannot be denied that some controversial announcements were made at that time – e.g. the increases in payments to councillors – and that Conservative party chairman David Davis urged a high-level investigation into the issue. Jo Moore resigned the following year and retrained as a teacher, but 'burying bad news' has passed into the language. **Verdict: Insensitive.**

14. Close the north (2008)

David Cameron was swift to distance himself from his favourite right-wing think tank Policy Exchange in August 2008 when they came out with what sounded, in a strong field, like the barmiest policy ever. Northern cities like Liverpool, Bradford and Sunderland were beyond help, argued the report (Scotland and Wales didn't seem to come into it) and instead of pouring regeneration money into them, we should instead be paying residents of the north to come to the south to live and work. Oxford and Cambridge, hilariously, were suggested as possible destinations. The north of England would, in this scenario, be left as some sort of post-apocalypse landscape stretching from the Watford Gap to Berwick-upon-Tweed, with the

---

* 'Epitaph for the eighties? "There is no such thing as society"' at http://briandeer.com/social/thatcher-society.htm

M1 overgrown with weeds, houses left to decay and feral whippets roaming wild. It's difficult not to wonder why this did not come out on 1 April, really. The authors of the report appeared in the media to defend it, arguing that they had not really said what they were alleged to have said and that they had wanted to open up a debate on regeneration. Anyone could see that no modern party was going to adopt this – there are plenty of Conservative voters in the north, after all, even if not many seats – and yet the left-wing bloggers and press crowed with delight about this having shown the 'true colours' of today's caring and sharing Tories. It didn't stick, and within a few days the idea was just one more silly-season story. Proof, then, that some ideas are a bit too right-wing even for the Conservatives. **Verdict: Ecky-*thump*!**

15. Go nuclear (1980s–present)

It seems like something from an edgy, paranoid age – the nuclear-crazed 1980s, when you were either pro or anti, when you were unilateral or multilateral, when you supported the Greenham Common women or laughed at them. Ronald Reagan was considered either the saviour of the free world, standing firm against the Evil Empire with his light-sabre of truth, or a mad old actor with his nervy finger on the nuclear button. The fear of the four-minute warning pervaded popular culture, from books to music videos. Labour's 1983 'suicide note' manifesto proposed unilateral disarmament and was laughed out of the ballot box. These days, everyone seems a little more equivocal on the whole thing, with the East–West arms race having supposedly calmed down and the case being made for the ongoing use of nuclear power. **Verdict: Not yet in meltdown.**

16. Tax junk food (2008)

One from France here. *Le Figaro* reported in August 2008 that a 'nutritional tax' on fatty foods was being considered.* You can almost imagine that catching on in the UK, with Jamie Oliver already advising the government on his 'pukka' brand of healthy eating, while armies of angry mums protest at the school gates while pushing pies and chips through the railings. **Verdict: Sacré bleu.**

17. Embrace Europe (1990s–present)

The one that tore the Conservative party apart in the 1990s, and doesn't look like going away. How close should our ties with our European neighbours be? Would the British people baulk at a federal Europe? Probably. Until the question is formally asked in a referendum, we will never know for certain – and oddly, successive governments keep finding good reasons not to ask it. It's almost as if they are frightened of what people might say. **Verdict: Hands across the water.**

18. Offer 'choice' in education (1990s–present)

School league tables, introduced by a Conservative administration and subsequently supported by Labour, are a desperate tool whose relevance continues to be baffling. School heads dislike them, teachers despair about them, children cannot see the point of them and parents wring their hands over them. The only people who actively seem to like them are the politicians, as they are just the kind of blunt instrument which appeals to people who value statistics over less measurable qualities. It baffles parents of school-age children why they are supposed

---

* Cited in GalliaWatch, http://galliawatch.blogspot.com/2008/08/taxation-frenzy.html

to covet 'choice', when what they want is simply a good local school and not a spurious 'choice' between a good one, a mediocre one and a bad one. 'Choice', the application of market forces to the one thing which should be free for all – education – distracts from the real issue, namely the need to improve educational standards across the board. And governments know this. That's why they like it. **Verdict: Could do better.**

19. Feed your daughter a BSE-burger (1990)

John Selwyn Gummer, the Conservative agriculture minister who took most of the flak for the BSE scandal, decided that he'd show the media his confidence in British beef. In May 1990, at a boat show in Suffolk, Mr Gummer paraded his four-year-old daughter Cordelia in front of the cameras and gave her a burger to munch. She didn't appear too keen, so it was up to the minister himself to have a bite later on for the media. It didn't do his cause any good, and it seems to be the one thing he's remembered for to this day. The beef with beef continued well into the New Labour era, with expert Dr Erik Millstone declaring himself 'seriously underwhelmed' with the government's handling of the issue. One can be sure a grown-up Cordelia is embarrassed by it all now. **Verdict: Fries with that?**

20. Apologise (2009)

Once the expenses scandal broke, it appeared there was to be no stopping the revelations. One after another, MPs came out of the woodwork, sheepishly declaring their Laura Ashley wallpaper, their John Lewis furniture and their dodgy DVDs, like naughty schoolboys who had been found smoking behind the bike sheds and couldn't really get away with pretending they hadn't. Some protested that what they had done was 'within the rules', conveniently ignoring the implication that, therefore, the rules needed revising. Apology seems to be the get-out clause of the moment – although, contrary to the suggestion in the Elton John song, it appears to be the easiest word for some to utter. Like five-year-old children, MPs have discovered that the S-word can often help them out of a jam. The public mood on the subject continues to ebb and flow, and while some of the more scandalous revelations may in time be forgotten, the body of MPs as a whole will take a long time to be forgiven. The reputation of Parliament may take a generation to recover. **Verdict: A sorry state.**

Voters will forgive us for many things, but engaging in an internal row that would make student faction-fighting look pretty cool is not one of them. Some Labour politicians should know better. Their excitable advisers clearly don't.

Labour back-bencher Jon Cruddas in 2008 – taking the moral high ground, but keeping a toe in the shark-infested waters

PolFax: Election Nuggets

- An Australian man called Geoff Richardson changed his full name to 'Of The Above None' and stood as an independent for the seat of Gilmore at the 2007 Australian federal election. On the ballot paper he appeared as 'NONE, Of The Above'.

- The general election in North Korea on 8 October 1962 recorded a 100 per cent turnout of electors – and a 100 per cent vote for the Workers' Party of Korea.

- The largest UK constituency in population terms is currently the Isle of Wight (which in the last twenty years has bounced between the Liberal Democrats and the Conservatives) with 110,000 on the electoral roll. The smallest is the Labour/SNP marginal seat Na h-Eileanan an Iar (formerly known as the Western Isles) with 21,000.

- A deposit for UK parliamentary elections was introduced in 1918 to discourage any non-serious candidates, and was then £150. A candidate had to gain 12.5 per cent of the vote to keep their deposit. It wasn't until 1985 that the deposit was increased to £500, and the threshold for keeping it was lowered to 5 per cent of the total vote.

- Charles Tennyson (uncle of the poet Alfred Lord Tennyson), who was elected as an MP in Grimsby for the first time in 1818, celebrated his victory by presenting a bottle of wine to the fathers of each of 92 children about to be christened.

- In 1972, Republican Richard Nixon became president of the USA with a landslide victory of 47,170,000 votes to the Democrat George McGovern's 29,170,000 – the greatest popular vote margin ever attained by a candidate in a US presidential election.

PolFax: Unparliamentary Language

Some inappropriate things MPs have called each other
in Parliament over the years:

'Fat bounder': How Labour MP Tony Banks described
then chancellor Nigel Lawson, when asking the Speaker
in 1997 if he had the power to haul him out of a dinner and into the House to give account of himself. Banks
amended the insult to 'corpulent right honourable gentleman' and asked, to general mirth, that he be 'brought
here in a tumbril'.*

'Squirt': Cantankerous Labour veteran Dennis Skinner
was once taken to task for referring to another MP in this
way. In fact, Dennis Skinner has been suspended from
the House on at least ten occasions!†

'Misleading': Gordon Brown received a request for 'tem-
perate language' from the Speaker (although no further action was taken) for saying that David Cameron
was being 'misleading' over the Gould report into the
Scottish elections in 2007.‡

**'Acting with the sensitivity of a sex-starved boa-
constrictor':** Banks again, describing Mrs Thatcher this
time. He seems to have got away with this one, too.§

'Dimwit': John Major, when prime minister, ascribed this
term to the then opposition leader Tony Blair. He was
asked to withdraw his remark.¶

---

* 'Wit and Wisdom of Tony Banks', *Independent*, 10 January 2006.
† *Hansard*, 2 July 1992: Column 956.
‡ *Hansard*, 24 October 2007: Column 291.
§ Tony Banks obituary, *Independent*, 9 January 2006.
¶ *Hansard*, 7 February 1995: Column 138.

'Liar': This is the biggie. That's the one thing you absolutely must not say, and Labour's Tam Dalyell overstepped the mark twice, both times with Mrs Thatcher. In fact, he rather seemed to relish calling her a 'sustained brazen deceiver ... a bounder, a liar, a deceiver, a cheat and a crook'.[*]

'Putting your penis in another man's arsehole': Not something an MP has accused another of doing, but this was the memorably colourful description of gay sex given by Tory MP Nicholas Fairburn in the 1994 age of consent debate.[†]

Drug references: Dennis Skinner (again) was banned from the Commons for a day for a jibe at George Osborne, which described the 1980s as a time when 'the only thing growing was the lines of coke in front of Boy George and the rest of the Tories'.[‡]

Other unacceptable terms are:

Blaggard
Coward
Git
Guttersnipe
Hooligan
Ignoramus
Rat
Swine
Stool-pigeon
Traitor

---

[*] *The Times*, 13 April 2005.
[†] *Hansard*, 21 February 1994: Column 98.
[‡] *Hansard*, 8 December 2005: Column 989.

One MP also may not refer to another as the 'dishon-ourable member for …', nor can they be called 'deceit-ful', 'hypocritical', 'dishonest' or 'misleading'. In the Chamber, one also cannot state of an MP that he or she has given a 'misstatement of truth'. However, there is a euphemism, first coined by Winston Churchill in 1906, which is acceptable: 'a terminological inexactitude'.

An MP also cannot imply that another MP is drunk, or refer to any use of illegal substances (see the Dennis Skinner/George Osborne example above).

If an MP makes a remark which the Speaker deems to be inappropriate, he or she is given the opportunity to withdraw it. Refusal to do so can result in the MP being 'named' – their name is read out by the Speaker and they must leave the Chamber.

———————————————

The Numbers Game: Top Ten

1: Times since 1945 that a party with a fully working majority has been replaced by another with a good enough majority to govern (in 1970, in case you are interested)

2: Candidates with surname 'Curran' in the 2008 Glasgow East by-election

3: Conservative Party leaders to have resigned since 1997 (Hague, Duncan Smith and Howard)

4: Sidney Webb's famous clause in the Labour party constitution, abolished in 1995 after much debate, symbolising a break with the past

5: Number of 'eco-towns' announced by Gordon Brown in 2007

6: Labour Party leaders who have become prime minister (Ramsay MacDonald, Attlee, Wilson, Callaghan, Blair and Brown)

7: Our historic rights, according to a combination of the Magna Carta and the 1689 Bill of Rights: equality under the law, no punishment without law, justice will not be denied or deferred, the right to lawful judgement by our peers, freedom of speech, freedom to elect a Member of Parliament and freedom from cruel or unusual punishments

8: Percentage lead taken by the SNP over Labour in Scotland in 2007, indicating the game was up

9: Points in Lord Fowler's 2008 plan for avoiding political suicide. These included telling the truth, re-establishing the importance of Parliament and the Cabinet, and not cosying up to the media

10: The PM's residence at Downing Street. The street is named after the soldier and diplomat Sir George Downing, and the PM's residence got its famous number in 1787 (after being number 5 for a while)

Vox Pops

People will say in six months' time, 'Wouldn't it be great to have that Blair back because we can't stand that Gordon Brown.'
David Miliband on *Question Time* in February 2007, apparently applying for both his fortune-teller's badge and the Boris Johnson Cup for Diplomacy.

5

Desperate Remedies:
Some disaster scenarios

*I have come to the conclusion that politics is too serious
a matter to be left to the politicians.*
Charles de Gaulle, president of the French Republic
1959–69

Sticking it to the enemy: the best
political betrayals

There's a great story of a new young MP coming into the
House for the first time, taking his seat and saying, as he
nodded across at the opposition benches: 'Well, at least
we get a good view of the enemy from here.' Winston
Churchill turned round and growled: 'No, my boy, that's
the opposition. The enemy is behind you.'*

It is one of the trickiest questions faced by the ambi-
tious politician – how to advance your own career, without raising the hackles of the person whose job you hope
to take. After all, any hint of conspiracy or disloyalty and
you're likely to be given the boot before you can do any
damage. One popular approach is to appear loyal and
allow your true intentions to be read into the gaps.

In contrast to the strife-ridden Tories of the 1990s,
New Labour emerged as a party in which all members
needed to be 'on message' and 'singing from the same

* Various versions quoted in a variety of sources, but see http://
www.abelard.org/abstracts/quotes5-churchill.php

hymn sheet'. In the early days, criticism of New Labourites tended to characterise them as robotic drones, instructed by their pagers direct from Alastair Campbell and Peter Mandelson, with the leadership anxious to ensure nobody broke ranks – which is why the occasions when Labour has managed an 'Et tu, Brute?' moment are all the more enjoyable. It's as if the real people beneath the pager-wielding clones have finally emerged, like 'sleeper' personalities.

In-fighting, backstabbing and party disloyalty might be cited as the kind of thing which puts people off politics, but they can be hugely entertaining. And on another level, they illustrate how politicians cannot really win – if they troop merrily into the Aye lobby, following the whips' commands like gently grazing sheep, they are accused of being toadies lacking in political fire or imagination, and yet if they dare to speak out against their party line, then that is illustrative, apparently, of how untrustworthy they all are.

Politics needs its colourful characters, and at times this means a less than harmonious working relationship. It's all part of the theatre. Here, for those who want to see how it's done, are some of the great political disloyalties and betrayals of our time.

2008: The Milibandwagon

Labour foreign secretary David Miliband's statement of 'support' for the embattled Gordon Brown in July 2008 is a prime example – writing in the *Guardian*, Miliband was ostensibly declaring that the party needed to unite and be more positive about pushing forward its agenda. Days of whispering were at an end – someone high-profile in the party had come out and said it in public.[*]

Little wonder that commentators refused to take his article at face value, and some backbenchers called for his resignation. Between the lines, the message was clear – it was a gauntlet, if not thrown down then at least carefully and politely placed on the floor, for the leadership. Nowhere in the article did Miliband mention Gordon Brown by name (he only expressed confidence in him when expressly asked a direct question at a press conference the following day). Every success cited by Miliband was one from the Blair era, and every weakness one which had been laid at Brown's door. 'When people hear exaggerated claims, either about failure or success, they switch off,' declared Miliband, with an acerbic precision which must have had the PM, on holiday in Southwold at the time, hurling his ice-cream into a rock pool. **Backstab Rating:** ⵏⵏⵏ

1999: The 'Tory Turncoat'

Shaun Woodward could hardly have seemed more Tory back in 1999. Married to an heiress (Camilla Sainsbury) and allegedly with his own butler, the MP for Witney raised eyebrows when he crossed the floor and joined the Labour government, the most high-profile defector of the time. Campaigning in 2001 to be the new Labour MP for St Helen's South, Woodward found himself the subject of a certain amount of media ridicule – but he stuck with Labour and was rewarded by becoming secretary of state for Northern Ireland. We note that he chooses not to receive a ministerial salary. **Backstab Rating:** ⵏⵏⵏ

---

[*] David Miliband, 'Against all odds we can still win, on a platform for change', *Guardian*, 29 July 2008.

2001: Having your cake, eating it, and having it again
Paul Marsden, elected Labour member for Frodsham
in Cheshire, left Labour in 2001 for the more orange
pastures of the Liberal Democrats over the question of
military action in Afghanistan. After announcing his
intention to leave politics in 2004, he then became the
first floor-crosser since Winston Churchill to cross back
– he rejoined Labour in 2005, saying: 'Whatever my past
feelings about Tony, whatever my past feelings about the
way I was treated – and I think I was treated badly at the
time – right now there is no point harking about the
past.'* **Backstab Rating:** ⚔⚔

2007: Another 'Tory Turncoat'
The day before the 'orderly transition' from Blair to
Brown in June 2007, former shadow Northern Ireland
secretary Quentin Davies (MP for Grantham and
Stamford) crossed the floor – delighting the Labourites
and resulting in Tories making snorting noises about how
he'd never really been one of them, anyway. Conservative
leader David Cameron's rather frosty reaction was: 'You
have made your choice and the British people will make
theirs.' This was at a time when Gordon Brown was making announcements (swiftly forgotten, as it turned out)
about creating a 'government of all the talents'. Perhaps
this was shown up as the embarrassing idea it was when
it was revealed that TV presenter Fiona Phillips had
been asked on board as an adviser, and had produced
a list of policy ideas including the banning of titles and
scrapping of the honours system, the end of selection in
schools, taking George W. Bush to Iraq to be shot, and

---

* Quoted in BBC Election 2005 News, http://news.bbc.co.uk/1/hi/
uk_politics/vote_2005/frontpage/4414967.stm

compulsory classes in bunting and cupcakes for stay-
at-home mums. Only one of the above is totally made
up. (Clue: it's not the George Bush one.) And far from
having a 'government of all the talents', Gordon Brown
found himself hard pressed, in the second year of his
premiership, to hold on to a cabinet of people who even
liked him a little bit. **Backstab Rating:** ⁄⁄

1990: The ambitious maverick

Regarded by some as the best leader the Conservative
party never had, Michael Heseltine famously mapped
out his career on the back of an envelope while at
Oxford ('Fifties: millionaire. Sixties: MP. Seventies: minister. Eighties: Cabinet. Nineties: Downing Street' – as
Meat Loaf almost sang, four out of five ain't bad). Mrs
Thatcher's verdict on him was that he was 'not one of
us' – and it was Heseltine's strong leadership challenge
in 1990 that told the 'Iron Lady' the game was finally up.
Backstab Rating: ⁄⁄⁄⁄

1969: Callaghan and *In Place of Strife*

In Place of Strife: a Policy for Industrial Relations was a famous
Government Command Paper of 1969, in which the
legendary Barbara Castle, secretary of state for employment and productivity, sought to draw up a new legislative framework for the trade unions which promised
to 'strengthen and improve industrial relations in this
country'.* Jim Callaghan, the home secretary at the time,
was one of the framework's leading opponents. Jump forward seven years, to 'Sunny Jim' leading the party and
the country, when the unreformed trade unions came
back to bite him in the famous Winter of Discontent – a

---

* *In Place of Strife*, Government Command Paper 3888, 1969.

time whose stories of unburied dead, bin bags piling up in the streets and industrial action are still dismissed as exaggerations by some on the Left (a stance rather belied by the obvious photographic and filmed evidence of the time). Callaghan, who could have called an election in October 1978, had famously dithered, and the months which followed led to his downfall and the election of Mrs Thatcher in 1979.

An unelected, somewhat plodding Labour prime minister – perhaps finding it hard to follow in the foot-steps of a charismatic, long-serving predecessor who had stood down part-way through a term – dithers over an autumn general election and slowly loses the goodwill of the people as the country descends into chaos, while appearing not to realise the scale of the calamity around him, before losing to a modernising Conservative who was somewhat unexpectedly elected as party leader a few years earlier … One should ask if history often repeats itself. **Backstab Rating:** \\\\\\

1995: The Euro-sceptic whisperings

With none of Thatcher's iron grip, the affable-but-dull John Major was portrayed in the media as a 'grey man'. He was taken to task by then leader of the opposition Tony Blair, who famously declared: 'I lead my party – he follows his!'* In an attempt to flush out what he had referred to off the record as the 'bastards' in his Cabinet, Major took the unusual step of resigning as leader – but not as prime minister – and seeking re-election, say-ing it was time for his detractors to 'put up or shut up'. Only the Euro-sceptic John Redwood took him up on the challenge, resigning as secretary of state for Wales

---

* *Hansard*, 25 April 1995: Column 656.

to challenge Major. The result was decisively enough in Major's favour for him to have seen off those cheeky Alan B'stards for the time being – 218 votes to 89, with two abstainers and twelve spoilt papers (wouldn't we love to know what was written on those?). And so Major now had the joy of two more years of a dwindling majority and growing public impatience with the Tories, finally fighting an election in 1997 which he knew he was going to lose. Once he did, of course, he seemed almost chipper, going off whistling into the sunset for some cricket-watching like a man who has had the weight of the world removed from his shoulders. **Backstab Rating:** ЖЖ

1959: 'Floorcross' Shawcross

'Crossing the floor' was originally used to mean voting against one's party, but has come to mean leaving the party altogether to join another. Famous for having been the Attorney General who brought the treacherous Lord Haw-Haw to justice, Hartley William Shawcross, having been a post-war Labour MP, sat in the House of Lords in 1959 as a cross-bencher and later expressed support for the SDP, leading to his nickname of 'Sir Shortly Floorcross'. Famous for difficult relationships with the press, he lambasted the *News of the World* without having read it, and made certain comments which today would be regarded as un-PC. He died in 2003. **Backstab Rating:** Ж

2003: The fate of the 'Quiet Man'

Iain Duncan Smith, or 'IDS', was the most put-upon Tory leader in recent memory, and was the victim not of an election defeat but – perhaps proving the Churchillian maxim that opened this chapter – of disquiet within his own party. Coming into the job after the resignation of William Hague in 2001, he'd never been widely expected to win – but win he did, after bookies' favourite Michael Portillo was ousted in the final MPs-only round and IDS topped a vote of the whole membership against the Euro-friendly Kenneth Clarke. Things didn't go well from the start, with Clarke describing Duncan Smith as attracting the 'lunatic fringe' and of being a 'hanger and flogger'.* With the party's poll ratings dipping below 30 per cent, Duncan Smith faced an uphill struggle – not least to make himself heard at the party conference. In a speech written by screenwriter Julian Fellowes, he famously declared: 'The quiet man is here to stay, and he's turning up the volume!'† Sadly, the party decided to change the channel. A vote of no confidence in IDS resulted in his resignation in October 2003 and, with MPs perhaps sensing that the party did not have the stomach for another divisive contest, Michael Howard was installed after a 'coronation'. Howard led the party to a slightly improved position in the 2005 general election before stepping down himself. IDS, though, has survived, and although the 'Quiet Man' tag follows him around, he continues to play a key role behind the scenes, chairing the Centre for Social Justice (an independent policy group). **Backstab Rating:** ⫚⫚⫚

2006: The One That Didn't

This one never happened. Before Mark Oaten's resignation from the Lib Dem front bench, a defection to the Tories was being mentioned in the blogosphere.

---

* Quoted by Douglas Fraser in the *Sunday Herald*, 2 September 2001.
† Iain Duncan Smith, speech to the 2003 Conservative party conference.

Whether Oaten, famously one of the engineers of the
Lib Dems' pro-free-market 'Orange Book' in 2004, was
seriously inclined to make such a move is open to debate.
In the light of the scandal that followed, David Cameron
is probably relieved he didn't. **Backstab Rating:** ⭤

Back to Basics

Most people seem to feel, these days, that a politician
should be entitled to a private life and that, as long as
what he or she is doing is legal, it shouldn't impact on
their ability to do their job.

In theory, this seems a sound notion, although it did
backfire somewhat in the 1990s when John Major decided
that the name of his new campaign was going to be 'Back
to Basics'. This was immediately seized upon – rightly or
wrongly – as a demand for a return to Victorian family
values, all of which was unfortunately undermined by a
series of tawdry sex scandals involving various Tory MPs
being caught in interesting situations (none of which
should concern us here).

And politicians' sexual orientation is far less of an
issue than it once was: a poll in 1998, days after agriculture minister Nick Brown was forced by a newspaper
exposé to admit his homosexuality, indicated that 52 per
cent of people thought being openly gay was compat-
ible with holding a Cabinet post.[*] Labour's Chris Smith
was the first openly gay Cabinet minister. Alan Duncan,
elected in 1992, was the Tories' first openly gay minister,
although he did not declare his sexuality publicly until
2002. However, writer Matthew Parris has said his answer
to the question of how many gay MPs there are in the

---

[*] ICM/*Guardian* poll, 1998.

House of Commons would be 'between five and two hundred, depending on what you mean'.*

Voters being more laid-back about MPs' sex lives could also be a result of a move towards a less judgmental culture in general – MPs are only human, and will still have the full range of human prejudices and preconceptions, but they tend not to lecture the public quite so much as they used to about what they should (or should not) get up to in the privacy of their own homes.

Even an admission (or non-denial) of youthful pot-smoking, something which could have killed a politician's career in the 1970s, is almost *de rigueur* for members of the Labour Cabinet these days. But it was perhaps surprising to some how easily David Cameron weathered the storm-in-a-bong over the drugs question. The media wrestled with it for a few days, realised it was going nowhere when he claimed the right to have had a 'normal student life' before politics, and left it there. Even a biography of Cameron serialised in the *Independent on Sunday*, in which he gave more specific admissions, didn't seem to harm his popularity.† The vast majority of voters seem unshockable on the subject now – at least, until and unless Amy Winehouse stands for Parliament and totters out on the stump with a bit of chemical assistance. And Elizabeth May, the leader of Canada's Green party, apologised in September 2008 for *not* having smoked pot when speaking about her proposals to legalise marijuana.‡ How times change ...

---

* Matthew Parris, 'Are you gay or straight? Admit it, you are most likely an in-between', *Daily Telegraph*, 5 August 2006.
† 'Yes, I took drugs, says Cameron', *Independent on Sunday*, 11 February 2007.
‡ Reuters, 17 September 2008.

Financial impropriety seems to concern people more, as recent controversies over MPs' expenses and the so-called 'John Lewis list' have shown. One imagines a good few constituents expostulating at the thought of their elected member claiming for a £795 Maestro leather sofa when most people's houses are furnished with cheap-and-cheerful Ikea furniture they have had to fund themselves. (Former chief whip Michael Jopling reportedly described Michael Heseltine as the kind of man who 'buys his own furniture', which was supposed to indicate that he was some kind of vulgar *nouveau-riche* arriviste.[*]) And the 'cash for questions' affair, in which some Tory MPs were said to have taken bribes in return for parliamentary questions, was one of the many storms weathered by the John Major government and the scandal eventually resulted in the establishment of the Committee on Standards in Public Life.[†]

Should I Stay Or Should I Go?
Memorable resignations

One interesting piece of trivia is that, technically, MPs haven't been able to 'resign' their seats voluntarily since 1623. They can only stop being an MP by a) death, which is understandably unpopular, b) elevation to the peerage, which they may not be ready for just yet, c) dissolution (end of a Parliament) or d) expulsion. So anyone no longer wishing to be an MP has to make themselves unable to be one. He/she must go through a formal process of applying for a paid office of the Crown, in order to become ineligible to sit as an MP (under the

Act of Settlement, passed in 1701). There are a couple to choose from: Crown Steward and Bailiff of the
Chiltern Hundreds, or Steward and Deputy Steward of
the Manor of Northstead. The positions are purely sine-
cures, and tend to be used alternately. The departing
MP will hold the position until officially released (David
Davis was released almost immediately in order to fight
his by-election).

But here we also have 'falling on one's sword', also
known as departing in order to spend more time with
the wife/mistress/pet newts. There is an easy way to
spot that a minister is about to get the push – the prime
minister goes on the record as saying that said minister
has 'his full support'. Two days later, the minister is out.
Everybody has known for about a week before that it was
going to happen, and it's been said in private – the only
person who wouldn't admit it was the minister himself.

Political leaders rarely go quietly or gracefully. Once
the whisperings begin, it's hard to see where they will
end – a leader either has to take immediate, firm control,
or slowly succumb as it slips out of their grip. Here are
some of the ways in which the great and the good – plus a
few of the also-rans – have left office over the years.

Margaret Thatcher (1990)

It seemed to many that she had been around forever. For
those in their teens and early twenties, she was perhaps
the first prime minister they had been properly aware of.
Nevertheless, everyone's time must come – and in the
end, it was her own party that did for the 'Iron Lady',
ousting her where two successive Labour leaders had
failed. Divisions over the poll tax and Europe had made
her position untenable. First there was the resignation

of Geoffrey Howe, then a leadership challenge from Michael Heseltine which he didn't win, but which was strong enough (152 of the 379 votes available) to let her know she probably wouldn't win the second round. And so, with a tear in her eye, Mrs T left Downing Street for the final time. A good few people shouted: 'Rejoice!' One would think her enemies would now be happy, but they have filled the subsequent two decades with ghoulish (and, indeed, somewhat childish) invective on the subject of her departure from this world. For some people, evidently, the 1980s are not yet over, and some on the Left seem incapable of enjoying the moral high ground in an adult manner. **Resign-ometer: 10/10**

Reforming from the centre: Paddy Ashdown (1999)

Stepped down as leader of the Lib Dems in 1999 after eleven years. When first elected MP for Yeovil in 1983, Ashdown had promised himself he would not do the job beyond his 60th birthday. And so he was off. Lord 'call me Paddy' Ashdown still turns up when the voice of a centrist elder statesman is required (and David Steel isn't available). **Resign-ometer: 7/10**

Wielding the knife, never wearing the crown: Michael Heseltine (1986)

'Tarzan' resigned from Margaret Thatcher's Cabinet over the Westland affair (a difference of opinion over a rescue bid for Britain's last helicopter company). Came back to haunt the 'Iron Lady' as the 'stalking horse' candidate who helped to bring her down in 1990. Becoming prime minister remains the only achievement unfulfilled on the list of goals made by the young Heseltine in the 1950s. **Resign-ometer: 9/10**

Ageism in action: Sir Menzies Campbell (2007)

Resigned as Lib Dem leader after just eighteen months, the media having continually made his seniority an issue. Amusingly, in July 2007 newly appointed PM Gordon Brown had referred to 'Ming' as the 'leader of the opposition', which had a lot of people muttering 'in his dreams'. **Resign-ometer: 6/10**

Setting the agenda: David Davis (2008)

Davis resigned from the Tory front bench in 2008 and fought a by-election in his seat of Haltemprice and Howden in order to put 42-day detention of terrorism suspects on the agenda – the jury is still out on how successful he was at doing so, but he was re-elected with over 70 per cent of the vote. Interestingly, the BBC's political correspondent Nick Robinson said that he had underestimated 'the extent to which the act of resigning on an issue of principle would elevate David Davis in the eyes of many in this profoundly anti-political age'.* **Resign-ometer: 5/10**

Early Labour setback: Ron Davies (1998)

Stepped down as secretary of state for Wales after an incident on Clapham Common in which he was mugged at knifepoint. At the time, this was seen as the Labour government's worst disaster since coming to office. Which in retrospect would be funny if it were not so desperately tragic. **Resign-ometer: 5/10**

---

* 'So who was right?' in Nick Robinson's Newslog, posted 11 July 2008: http://www.bbc.co.uk/blogs/nickrobinson/2008/07/so_who_was_righ.html

Mid-life crisis: Mark Oaten (2006)

This one had everything – sex, scandal and the Lib Dems. Oaten, famously the victor in the Winchester seat after upping a majority of just two to over 20,000, had risen through the ranks to be the Liberal Democrats' home affairs spokesman, but it was affairs slightly closer to home which would embarrass him into resigning from the party leadership election and his brief. Oaten was apparently having a mid-life crisis over his premature baldness, and the shenanigans reported luridly at the time brought him into disrepute. Rehabilitation as a media pundit, however, is not to be ruled out. **Resign-ometer: 7/10**

A matter of perception: David Blunkett (2004)

An email was made public showing a visa application for the then home secretary's ex-lover's nanny, which had said 'no favours but slightly quicker'. Mr Blunkett claimed to be unaware of the email's contents and insisted he had done nothing wrong, but resigned in case there was a 'perception' that he had – a fine point, some might say. In charge of Sheffield in the 1970s when the Red Flag flew over the Town Hall – some think this was a metaphor, but it was literally true – the former home secretary is still (perhaps bafflingly) popular in his home city. **Resign-ometer: 8/10**

The 'grey man': John Major (1995)

John Major resigned in 1995 to oust those he'd privately called the 'bastards' from his Cabinet, to see if anyone would dare move against him. John 'the Vulcan' Redwood, Welsh secretary at the time (the one who was seen nodding his head in an 'oh, God, please let this be over' kind of way to the Welsh national anthem) famously did, and gained enough votes to damage Major without it being enough to prompt him to resign – or, if you prefer, Major won just comfortably enough for him to silence the critics and remain in office for another two years. Michael Portillo, widely expected to stand against Major – to the point where he had commandeered a campaign HQ and installed a number of telephone lines – eventually didn't seize the moment. After losing his seat in one of the most famous moments of the 1997 election, Portillo settled for a life of documentary-making and acerbic (yet cosy) comments on the *This Week* sofa alongside Hackney MP Diane Abbott. **Resign-ometer: 8/10**

The sheep that roared: Geoffrey Howe (1990)

Howe's resignation in 1990 as deputy prime minister is thought to have been one of the factors hastening Thatcher's own departure. Her approach to policy on Europe, he said, was 'rather like sending your opening batsmen to the crease, only for them to find, as the first balls are being bowled, that their bats have been broken before the game by the team captain'.* Bowled out for six. The *Independent* praised his 'dogged integrity and patient decency', but the quote most people remember about Howe is from Labour chancellor Denis Healey, who likened criticism from him to 'being attacked by a dead sheep'. Handbags at dawn, gentlemen. **Resign-ometer: 8/10**

Fighting, not quitting: Peter Mandelson (2001)

Slippery spin doctor Mandelson left the Cabinet for the second time in January 2001, following a controversy over

---

* *Hansard*, 13 November 1990: Column 464.

the passport application for Indian billionaire Srichand Hinduja – but denied he had done anything wrong. Six months later at the general election, Mandelson was returned as MP for Hartlepool. He gave the most extraordinary victory speech – his macho declaration: 'I'm a fighter, not a quitter' drew, it's fair to say, a mixed response. His return to the Cabinet in 2008 was one of the biggest surprises Gordon Brown has sprung so far. **Resign-ometer: 8/10**

Outside the tent: Norman Lamont (1993)

Apparently Lamont offered to resign as chancellor after the 1992 Black Wednesday fiasco but 'not too insistently', whatever that means. A few months later he was effectively removed by being offered, in a frosty exchange, the post of environment secretary instead, which Prime Minister John Major probably knew he'd turn down. Lamont famously described the Major government as giving the impression of being 'in office but not in power'. The two men have since made up. 'We went to lunch,' says Lamont. 'All was harmony. These things run out of steam. It was a long time ago. You can't go through life brooding about these things.'* (Except, apparently, if you hated Mrs Thatcher.) **Resign-ometer: 7/10**

Renaissance man: William Hague (2001)

Following a bruising (if terminally dull) election campaign in 2001, one whose result everybody knew before it happened, the leader of one of the least effective oppositions in modern political history fell on his sword in the early hours of the morning after the election. To be fair,

---

* Interviewed by William Keegan and Alex Brett in the *Observer*, 22 July 2007.

the witty and erudite Hague had often had Tony Blair on the back foot in Prime Minister's Question Time, and always had better jokes. They just didn't translate into votes. Resignation, though, has turned out to be a good career move, with Hague's position as shadow foreign secretary almost seeming a casual diversion from his lucrative business of after-dinner speaking and biography writing. One senses he will be a survivor. **Resign-ometer: 8/10**

Oops: an entire parish council (2002)

The entire parish council of Aiskew in North Yorkshire resigned over the 'Parish Councils (Model Code of Conduct) Act', which required parish councillors to reveal details of shareholdings in local businesses of over £25,000. **Resign-ometer: 6/10**

Honesty the best policy: Charles Kennedy (2006)

The Liberal Democrat leader denied his struggle with alcoholism for as long as he reasonably could, but then won admiration for bravely admitting it to the press; his subsequent withdrawal from the party leadership race seemed more of a gracious admission of defeat than a humiliating climbdown, and he is still one of the most popular politicians with the general public. **Resign-ometer: 7/10**

Know when you're finally beaten: Neil Kinnock (1992)

Fated forever to have that moment when he lost his footing on Brighton beach replayed every time he slipped up, Neil Kinnock finally found that pride comes before a fall in 1992. It really looked as if the Labour party was going to win – the scrag-end of a struggling Tory administration had kicked out the 'bogeywoman' and replaced her with 'grey man' Major, and Kinnock had wrested back control of his own party by kicking out the troublesome Militants, a vocal minority group in the Labour party whose politics owed much to Marx and Trotsky. Even the BBC's exit polls predicted a Labour victory. When the unexpected news trickled in that the Tories had, in fact, hung on to power for a fourth term by a very slim majority, everyone was surprised. Kinnock stepped down three days later, blaming the Tory-friendly press, and in 1995 he joined the European Commission, later becoming its vice-president before retiring and taking up a seat in the House of Lords. **Resign-ometer: 7/10**

Into the sunset: Tony Blair (2007)

A bizarre, low-key departure for the most successful Labour prime minister ever. Murmurings about Blair's departure had been growing ever since Labour's second term, thanks to the so-called 'Granita deal' (named after the restaurant in which Blair and Gordon Brown supposedly agreed that the former would hand over the reins to the latter if Labour won more than once). And Gordon was kept waiting ... and waiting. Finally – perhaps not entirely in the manner of his own choosing, but certainly in a more controlled and stage-managed way than Mrs Thatcher had – Blair left office in June 2007. As if it wasn't odd enough for him to receive a standing ovation in the House of Commons – even from the opposition benches – the cameras followed him as he caught the train back up to his Sedgefield constituency, capturing the strangeness of one of the world's most important men reduced, albeit temporarily, to a mere backbencher. Blair resigned his Sedgefield seat almost immediately and it was retained by Labour in the subsequent by-election (much to Gordon Brown's relief, no doubt – starting to lose safe Labour seats really would never do). **Resign-ometer: 9/10**

The grand gesture: 85 members of the Pakistani opposition (2007)

In October 2007, 85 members of the opposition in Pakistan's parliament resigned in an attempt to deny any legitimacy to President Musharraf's attempt to be re-elected. **Resign-ometer: 7/10**

PolFax: Women in Parliament

- Women were first allowed to stand as MPs at Westminster in 1918.

- The first woman to be elected to the UK Parliament was the Anglo-Irish Countess de Markievicz, who, as a member of Sinn Féin, stood for election while in prison and did not take her seat. The first woman to sit in Parliament was Nancy Astor, in 1919.

- Most women over 30 gained the right to vote in 1918, but it was not until 1928 that women gained the same voting rights as men, with the passing of the Equal Franchise Act.

- Before 1997, there were more male MPs called John than there were female MPs.

- The number of female MPs went up from 63 to 120 in 1997, mainly thanks to Labour candidates – the so-called 'Blair's Babes'.

- In 2006, research by the Equal Opportunities Commission and equality campaigners the Fawcett Society revealed that voter turnout went up in seats where a female candidate was on offer.[*]

- Between 1918 and 2001, a total of 4,500 MPs sat in Westminster – and 240 of them, just 5 per cent, were women.

- The Electoral Reform Society gave a gloomy forecast for the future of female MPs in 2008, predicting that, at best, 22.9 per cent of MPs would be women at the next election – and that figure hangs on the increasingly unlikely outcome of a swing to Labour. The worst case scenario for future female parliamentarians is a Conservative working majority, which would give them only 18.5 per cent representation. Ken Ritchie, the Society's chief executive, said: 'The modest numbers of women in Parliament have been taken as a permanent breakthrough. In place of an upward curve we have seen a plateau, in what remains a male dominated institution.'[†]

- The cabinet chosen by Spain's prime minister José Luis Rodriguez Zapatero in April 2008 contained nine female ministers – making it the first Spanish cabinet in which women outnumbered men. These included Carme Chacón, Spain's first ever female defence minister.

---

[*] 'Choose a Winner, Select a Woman.' Joint response from the Equal Opportunities Commission and Fawcett Society press release, 2006. http://www.fawcettsociety.org.uk/documents/Women_MPs_increase_turnout.pdf

[†] Electoral Reform Society. http://www.electoral-reform.org.uk

Election Year Female MPs elected in UK

1945	24
1950	21
1951	17
1955	24
1959	25
1964	29
1966	26
1970	26
1974 (February)	23
1974 (October)	27
1979	19
1983	23
1987	41
1992	60
1997	120
2001	118
2005	128

The Numbers Game: The Pollsters

- 46 per cent: Respondents to a poll in Russia who opposed the cancellation of the 'against all candidates' option on the ballot paper from 2006. 42 per cent agreed that it was the right decision. Twelve per cent said it was 'hard to answer'[*]

- 23 per cent: Labour support in the *Daily Telegraph/* YouGov poll of May 2008. Under Michael Foot, supposedly the least popular leader the Labour party has ever had, the lowest they ever polled was 23.5 per cent[†]

[*] 'Elections and the "Against All Candidates" Choice' http:// bd.english.fom.ru/report/map/az/0-9/edomt0624_3/ed062422
[†] 'Gordon Brown support slumps to its lowest since polling began', *Daily Telegraph*, 30 May 2008.

- 75 per cent: In a 2008 *Guardian*/ICM poll, proportion of people who voted Labour in 2005 who said they now thought that Tony Blair had been a better prime minister than Gordon Brown[*]
- 20 per cent: Proportion of Tory voters who said in August 2008 that they would consider switching to Labour if Gordon Brown were replaced[†]
- 49 per cent: Proportion of people in UK who oppose compulsory voting, according to an Electoral Commission survey in 2007[‡]

Vox Pops

It's the froth versus the fundamentals – and I will continue concentrating on the fundamentals.

Tony Blair on 'cappuccino politics' in 2000

---

[*] 'Labour's poll rating worst since Thatcher', *Guardian*, 20 May 2008.
[†] YouGov poll, http://ukpollingreport.co.uk/blog/archives/1282
[‡] Cited in Suzy Dean, 'Compulsory voting: a smokescreen for disengagement', at http://www.culturewars.org.uk/2007-09/cvoting.htm

6

Media and Messages: The speaking and listening politician

I became politicised because the people in the coal-mining villages who were involved in the struggle knew why they were there. But they couldn't understand why some pop star from London would want to be there.
Billy Bragg (b. 1957), singer/songwriter and activist

The changing face of politics: the medium and the message

A time-traveller from 1994, the year not so long ago in which John Smith died and was replaced as Labour leader by Tony Blair, would have difficulty recognising the media landscape of today. Thanks to the internet, we live in an age of the democratisation of information, although it is also one in which the circumspect need to check their sources more than ever. There is now a plethora of political websites and blogs, both professional and amateur. At the 2005 general election, broadband hadn't quite taken off, so it will be interesting to see how the new global village responds to the next UK general election. Let's have a look at the strange relationship between politicians and the various media.

> *The story of how we managed the media in the end became*
> *something of significance in itself.*
>
> Tony Blair's communications director
> Alastair Campbell in 2002

There's an old clip of Margaret Thatcher in a radio studio with Robin Day, putting her headphones on to answer a call from a listener. For a moment she looks around, confused, unsure where this person is. It is as if, for a moment, all media have become some kind of magic force by which the ordinary person connects with the politician, and Maggie genuinely expected the questioner to float into view there and then in front of her. Or maybe she had already done so many interviews that day that she forgot whether she was on the radio or on television.

Harold Wilson seemed to love the media, to the extent of having his own chat show, and if he was around today would probably embrace the internet with chuckling glee. David Cameron took it one step further – one might almost say too far – with his early carefully staged 'webcameron' clips filmed at his home, in which he gave the cleaning lady the day off and did the washing-up as the children played quietly in the background, while Dave mused soberly on reducing the tax burden and lessening state intervention. We looked forward to future instalments, in which Dave dons a pinny and gets the cobwebs down from the corners with a feather duster while finding innovative ways of reducing Third World debt, and then uses the school run to come up with enticing new approaches to private-public partnership, but so far in vain.

The 'Iron Lady' didn't seem to mind laying herself open to the honest questioning of kids – Maggie did a couple of stints on Saturday morning TV. Maybe she was a little uncomfortable with the stream of inane banter, the endless irreverent chatter, the heckling and the interruptions – so she could always console herself by escaping from Prime Minister's Questions and appearing on *Saturday Superstore*. Subsequent prime ministers don't seem to have been as keen, which is a shame: the potential entertainment value of seeing Tony Blair gunged on *Jungle Run* or Gordon Brown playing *Hider in the House* is not to be underestimated. It is irresistible, indeed, to imagine such a suggestion being put to Brown, and how dour his reaction might have been.

'Media training' has a lot to answer for. These days, politicians expect to do TV and radio interviews as a matter of course, and are ready to use them for their own platform regardless of the actual question put to them or the issue under discussion. Not everyone can be as telegenic as James Purnell, who as secretary of state for work and pensions did an astonishing bilingual slot on the French TV channel France-24 in May 2008, nor guaranteed to be as bristlingly combative as Respect MP George Galloway or Labour maverick Bob Marshall-Andrews. The Liberal Democrats, meanwhile, do a good line in putting their young female members in the firing line, with the likes of Sarah Teather, Julia Goldsworthy and Jo Swinson deflecting questions with schoolmistressly charm.

There is an ongoing debate about whether the combative style adopted by questioners such as *Today*'s John Humphrys and *Newsnight*'s Jeremy Paxman encourages 'defensive play' in politicians, leading them to be less open than they otherwise would be. There is a fine line between assertiveness and aggression, and it is one which is carefully walked by *Question Time*'s David Dimbleby, who uses both humour and authority to rein in a guest who has decided to ramble on in their own direction.

So, for those inspired by this book to take up a political career, here are the best ways of turning the interview round to your advantage.

Ways to avoid answering the question

1. Trade statistics

'I think you'll find that, if we examine the facts, violent crime has actually gone down overall by 5 per cent, and the rate of decrease of violent crime has been faster than the decrease of violent crime under the previous government. So in fact, even though you were stabbed, you can rest assured that it would have been ever more likely ten years ago. And we have, in fact, just invested six squillion pounds in a new programme of knife crime risk assessment, the findings of which will be made available in two years' time.' This kind of thing is inevitable. Politicians have to deal in the facts available, and it is safe ground to reiterate what has been spent, and where it has been spent. Interviewers take delight in getting them onto rockier ground, and it's not surprising that politicians will try to stay off it.

2. Count the money twice

Another trick is to announce some spending which has already been announced as if it were something new, or to count the expenditure more than once in order to make it appear more than it actually is. Or to change the way you calculate something – so that the government could announce, for example, in mid-2008 that an inflation figure of 3.8 per cent is nothing to worry about as it's not as bad as that in America or elsewhere in Europe (conveniently ignoring the fact that, after coming to power, they changed the way in which inflation was calculated in order to remove two of people's biggest expenses – housing costs and council tax). Again, it's difficult to avoid doing this, given that it's an accepted trick.

3. Blame the other lot

'This hospital closure is part of a staged, careful process of restructuring within the NHS, and we certainly won't be taking any lessons on health provision from a government which wanted to send children back up chimneys, and which systematically culled anybody over the age of 60 who was looking a bit peaky.' You can get away with this for, probably, about two years before it stops looking merely spiteful and seems a little daft. Five years is pushing it.

4. Get on to another subject

'The subject of school closures is a very interesting point and it deserves to be dealt with at greater length. But could I just say that, without the consistent and careful investment we have made in maternity care, you wouldn't even have any children to be going to school in the first place.' Steering the interview is a skill used by many a skilled politician, and should not be underestimated as a tactic.

5. Waffle and prattle

'Well, that is a very interesting question, Jeremy, and I feel this post office closure needs to be examined within the wider context of the overall scheme of restructuring of the post office system. I think that my constituents will find, overall, when using the seasonally adjusted measure, that they are actually 29 per cent more likely under the restructured system to use a post office on days when they would not previously have done so. And, if we take into account the changes in parish boundaries, they have, in fact, more access to post office services per head of population per square mile than a comparably sized area of, for example, Orkney.'

6. Exude optimism

'John, if I could just come back on this question of the supposed imminent recession. While on holiday in Skeggington-under-Wold this summer – supporting the British tourist industry, if I may say so, unlike my Conservative counterpart who chose to take his family for an all-expenses-paid jaunt to Meat Loaf's luxury villa in the Seychelles – I noticed that the ice cream vendor was doing a roaring trade. When I questioned him, he was able to tell me that he had experienced a relatively quiet period in sales from November to April, and yet from May to August of this year he had encountered a real terms increase in unit sales of ice cream. But, of course, the media are only interested in pessimistic reporting.'

Economical with the truth?

All of the above may come across as slightly unfair to politicians, so it's useful to put them into some kind of context.

The phrase 'economical with the truth' has its origins in the eighteenth century but was popularised during the 1986 *Spycatcher* trial in Australia (the British government took legal action to attempt to prevent the publication of *Spycatcher*, the memoirs of the former MI5 agent Peter Wright). It's passed into the language now to refer to any politician who is being, shall we say, less than totally open with the public – which some would say means all of them. Yet another reason given for people's disillusionment with modern politics.

So, in this book's spirit of enthusing you about politics rather than making you more cynical, put yourself in their shoes for a minute. As minister for drawing pins, you've been hauled on to the *Today* programme in the middle of the government's biggest ever stationery crisis. John Humphrys is glowering at you across the mike, demanding to know why stationery prices are rocketing and queues at stationery counters around the country are growing by the minute. The minister for pens has conveniently made herself unavailable (still sulking at not having been in this year's Most Fanciable MPs list) and the minister for paper is holed up in his office, not taking calls. Any hope of getting the secretary of state for the Department of Stationery and Office Equipment on the line is a joke.

It's you that has to sit in the hot seat and squirm. And frankly, you know it's a major cock-up. You've been briefed, and you know more or less what to say to make things sound not quite as bad as they are. The style of questioning, though – and why not, as he has a job to do too – is on the aggressive side of probing. You know that if you tell the *complete* truth, you, the government and the stationery industry will all be in deep trouble more quickly than you can say 'Basildon Bond'.

So you try your best to limit the damage. You're not exactly going to stuff your leader on live radio – that would be seen as disloyal, and even though the public claim to like politicians who speak their minds, they are surprisingly intolerant of direct nastiness. And yet toeing the party line is interpreted as an attempt to safeguard your own job – when there might be an element of that, but you don't want to make things worse during a major national stationery crisis. You can't really win.

The Game

Honesty is seen as a virtue. But politics is a game, and it's one in which journalists are complicit. Politicians obviously *want* to be honest as much as they possibly can – no, don't snigger. It's just that, sometimes, the situations they find themselves in with interviewers mean that a direct, up-front honest answer would get them into hot water, and would possibly derail a policy before it's really got off the ground. There's no point being the person who pre-empts the official announcement, sending his colleagues into a flap – it just looks unprofessional. So questions need to be batted off with 'we currently have no plans', or 'we are investigating all possibilities', or 'we will be in a position to formulate our policy at the appropriate time'. All of which sounds like bluster. And may well be. But it could be better than causing an implosion.

Glen Newey of the University of Strathclyde postulated in 2003 the interesting theory that there is now a 'culture of suspicion' – in an information-hungry age, the electorate feels it has a right to know more than ever, and so politicians cannot get away with skimming over difficult questions as they used to.* This makes it sound

---

* 'Truth and Deception in Democratic Politics', study conducted by Dr Glen Newey at the University of Strathclyde Department of Government in Glasgow, 2003.

very much as if it's our fault for being an engaged electorate, but the point still seems valid. Can we be satisfied
with a limited amount of probing? Can we know when
enough is enough, and be aware that any more detailed
questioning is going to push the politician into a situation where they either have to a) be evasive or b) lie? It's
an ongoing consideration.

There is also the question of politicians wanting
the truth to come out, but at a time *suitable for them.* All
politicians like to set the agenda, not follow it. Michael
Heseltine famously said that he 'could not conceive of
a situation' in which he'd challenge Mrs Thatcher for
the Conservative leadership, but of course he did so, in
1990 – arguing that a situation had then arisen which he
could not have conceived of. One can have doubts, obviously – Heseltine is an intelligent and imaginative chap,
and so the idea that he could never have foreseen a time
when Mrs T would be vulnerable seems faintly prepos-
terous. But, of course, he avoided a lie. David Miliband
performed similar dances with the media in 2008 over
the question of his 'leadership challenge'.

So it's actually not that common for a politician to tell
a total, *outright* lie. One which will get them into trouble
by coming back and biting them. Look what happened
to Jonathan Aitken, imprisoned for eighteen months for
perjury – he's still infamous, and will bear the label 'disgraced former Cabinet minister' for the rest of his life.
He didn't help his case by pontificating about 'the simple
sword of truth and the trusty shield of British fair play',
but there can be few politicians who'd want to find themselves in his position.

The problem is that it is not possible, much as one
might wish it, to be utterly honest all of the time. A

politician who was always totally honest might be a liability for his party and for the country. 'Yes, actually, we
are really worried at the Treasury about these latest figures. They do look awful, don't they? I imagine people in
some parts of Manchester will be living in coal bunkers
and eating gruel within six months. It's got that bad.' Or:
'Well, yes, the terror threat is looking pretty grim. Central
London almost got blown up three times last year and
the security services only prevented it through a decent
tip-off just in time.' Or, in answer to the question: 'Do
you think the prime minister is doing a good job?' you'd
get: 'No, he's a smarmy and venal git who has derailed
every reforming measure I've tried to get through, and
the sooner he goes, the better. In fact, the men in grey
suits are gathering right now, and we'll have him out by
the autumn ...'

It would be refreshing, for a while. But after a few
months of this, would you not start to get a bit uneasy?
The whole process of government would fall apart if they
were always squabbling in public, and if we got to see
the internal arguments which led to the compromise
position for which the Cabinet went on to take collective
responsibility.

So, be careful what you wish for.

Becoming prime minister – and being liked?

When Barack Obama met Gordon Brown in the summer
of 2008, he had some words of comfort for the embattled PM, telling him that people always liked politicians
before they were in charge and rarely did so afterwards.
It's true that we have a long and noble tradition in the
UK of knocking our leaders down once we've set them

up – Americans don't quite get this, as there is more 'respect for the office' of president over there, which is simply not mirrored in our attitudes towards the prime minister (he/she is not our head of state, of course, and represents their party, not the country as a whole).

Being prime minister is an extraordinarily difficult job, and you can't really do it if your aim in life is to be popular. It's no coincidence that we often hear governments defending their 'difficult' decisions.

'Popularity', though, is a difficult one to judge, and history provides us with some paradoxical juxtapositions. Tony Blair was elected for the third time, with a comfortable (if not overwhelming) majority, only two years after sanctioning one of the most unpopular pieces of foreign policy in living memory, namely the involvement of British troops in the Iraq conflict. Margaret Thatcher also got elected three times despite being a deeply divisive figure. In both cases one can point to both a political system which allows a party into government even when the majority of votes are against them (Thatcher's highest ever percentage of the popular vote was 44 per cent in 1979, Blair's 43 per cent in 1997) and the decidedly shaky nature of the alternatives on offer at the time. In 2005, Blair was elected on a record low percentage of the vote – just 35 per cent.

So many factors come into play in British elections – this is not (or should not be) a 'presidential' vote where we mark our cross for an individual leader of the country. People vote for local MPs, and so may well support their local candidate even if they don't have much stomach for the party leader. In some parts of the country, they weigh the Labour vote – in others, as people often say, a donkey in a blue rosette would get elected.

The Colgate smile: the camera never lies

The *Independent*, reporting on the French presidential campaign in January 2007, noted that the frontrunners' New Year greetings posted on the internet differed markedly. Madame Royal, we were told, 'appears in a relaxed, amateur-style video', while Monsieur Sarkozy stood 'wearing a dark suit in front of the symbol of his UMP Party' and was 'fidgeting like a hyperactive child'.*

This kind of thing is typical of media reporting of politics – the relentless drip, drip, drip of visual imagery, of association, of implication and hint. Eventually, the media narrative takes hold and swings itself around, so that it appears to have been wrested from the media by the public and they think they are controlling it. Nicknames pass into popular culture – 'Phoney Tony' Blair, Maggie the 'Iron Lady', 'Sunny Jim' Callaghan. References to incidents come to be described in iconic, almost metaphorical ways, such as the 'baseball cap moment' of which William Hague was guilty.

Your newspaper and you

Supposedly, your choice of newspaper says a lot about you. This sweeping generalisation doesn't take account of people who want serious news but who may also peruse the *Sun* website as a guilty pleasure. It's perfectly possible to be interested in both the developments in the G8 summit and *The X Factor*, or to be following the latest marginal by-election while simultaneously monitoring the downward spiral of various self-destructive celebrities.

Although if your first reaction to the BBC's headline for the big terrorism story of March 2006, 'Jordan

---

* 'Style separates French hopefuls', *Independent*, 2 January 2007.

thwarts Al-Qaeda attack', was to wonder: 'Did she ward them off with her breasts?' then the chances are that you have spent too long reading *Heat* magazine and not long enough in the company of serious newspapers.

Here's a brief run-down on what you can expect to see printed on 'tomorrow's chip paper'.

The *Sun*

'It was the Sun wot won it.' Smug, self-satisfied and unashamedly populist – those were the words with which the country's most-read newspaper announced its hand in the narrow victory of John Major in 1992. Major had squeaked home in an election many had expected him to lose, and the country's favourite tabloid was determined to wring every last inch of copy out of the occasion.

The *Sun* had carried out a fairly *ad hominem* campaign against Neil Kinnock, Labour leader at the time, which reached its zenith with the front page headline: 'If Kinnock wins today will the last person to leave Britain please turn out the lights,' together with a picture of Kinnock's face superimposed over a light bulb. That headline is cited as a pivotal moment, maybe symbolic of, rather than instrumental in, the swing against Labour – along with a rather over-enthusiastic Sheffield stadium rally in which Kinnock addressed the masses like a rock star ('We're *all-raaaaaat!*' – still painful to watch). In contrast, 'Honest John' Major, unbowed by the public image of him as the 'Grey Man', took to the streets with a soapbox and loudhailer, happily getting down to street level and confronting the hecklers.

Only five years later, the paper was backing Tony Blair, declaring:

This is the election for the millennium. In six weeks'
time, Britain will vote for a government to take it into
the twenty-first century. The people need a leader with
vision, purpose and courage who can inspire them and
fire their imaginations. The *Sun* believes that man is
Tony Blair.*

William Hague, meanwhile, was pilloried in 1998 as a
'dead parrot' leading a moribund party – but a year on,
Hague's scepticism on the single European currency
found more sympathy with then-editor David Yelland
and his readers.

    Sun readers are generally thought to be less interested
in 'politics' generally than *Mirror* readers (although as we
have seen elsewhere, this idea of 'politics' in the abstract
can be misleading) – and, interestingly, less committed
to one particular party. It's not surprising that the paper
is seen as reflecting the mood of the nation, and that it's
often said that Rupert Murdoch, as the paper's owner,
has the power to influence elections decisively.

The *Mirror*

Unlike the fickle *Sun*, the *Daily Mirror* has always supported the Labour party through thick and thin since
1945, and is renowned for employing the left-wing inves-
tigative reporter Paul Foot. It was vociferous in its con-
demnation of the 2003 Iraq invasion and has consistently
taken an anti-George W. Bush stance. If you're a working-
class Labour voter, chances are this will be your newspaper of choice. And some of the middle classes read it too,
probably in a spirit of irony – especially when England is
in a major football tournament and every other story is

---

* *Sun*, 18 March 1997.

banished to the inside pages. They may be less tolerant of the paper's annual summer obsession with *Big Brother*, in which the population's priorities are writ large: Chaz, Shantelle and Twinkie (or whatever this year's bunch happen to be called) are well known enough to be referred to by first name or nickname only, while only a handful of high-profile politicians (Maggie, Two-Jags, Hezza) are accorded this privilege.

The *Grauniad*

No apologies for nicknaming the supposedly misprint-prone broadsheet of the leftie chattering classes. But to its credit, the *Guardian* is always anxious to fix inaccuracies when they appear, and has a regular Corrections and Clarifications column. Although latterly a 'critical friend' of the Labour government, the *Guardian* couldn't help itself gushing on the first anniversary of the Blair administration, remarking on 1 May 1998:

> Tony Blair and his team have made much more than a flying start. They have notched up perhaps the most successful first year of any administration in British political history. Their achievements range from the detail of policy to the more abstract terrain of leadership and national mood. Labour can congratulate itself on a golden year.*

In the light of what came later, you may find yourself involuntarily wincing at this. Other traits inclined to haul the more critical *Grauniad* reader up a bit include:

---

* *Guardian*, 9 May 1998.

- Juxtaposing right-on articles about the exploitation of women's bodies in the modelling industry with, on the very next page, adverts for overpriced beauty products
- Slipping two-page adverts for gas-guzzling 4×4s into the middle of articles about how we should all be terribly worried about climate change
- Filling its *Weekend* section with adverts for charming little leather handbags and hand-woven rattan footstools which one can buy from lovely little Kensington boutiques for only £259
- Running features on Islington couples called Inigo and Jocasta who have turned a row of three terraced houses into a minimalist glass palace with chrome staircases, whose living area appears to contain nothing but a leaf-shaped wooden bowl and a blue crystal orb, plus three artfully placed wooden bricks to suggest the presence of their children, Jago and Lysander
- Running the 'Let's Move To' column, often daring to feature northern towns and apparently researched on the internet by a journalist who has not ventured any further north than Camden and who describes local state schools with the empty adjective 'improving'.

One could go on. The *Grauniad* is that terribly nice, earnest, well-meaning, muesli-eating, vegetarian, animal-loving friend at work who has the eagerness of a small puppy and the politics of the Junior Common Room, who you sometimes want to hug and sometimes really, really want to smack.

The *Observer* is its Sunday cousin, which goes even lighter on the socialism and even heavier on the champagne and interior décor.

The *Daily Mail*

Beloved organ of Middle England and supporter of the 'common-sense' Right, giving gainful employment to, among others, Richard Littlejohn and former spin doctor Amanda Platell. The *Mail* (affectionately known as the *Hate Mail* by liberal opponents) is these days almost a parody of itself. As a 'critical friend' of the Conservative party, it was initially uncertain about Blair, who seemed like the kind of clean-cut politician its conservative readers would like. It didn't take long, though, for the *Mail* to revert to form, and in David Cameron it now has its own young, sharp-suited poster boy who they can at least plausibly pretend is right-wing. The *Mail* boasts the Conservative party's second-biggest readership after the *Telegraph*.

News is a secondary consideration for the *Mail*. Its readers will largely be working, homeowning members of the lower-middle and middle classes, who look to the august organ to provide their daily dose of scare stories about falling house prices and hook-wielding asylum seekers, tales of celebrities who have lost weight (especially if they can later bitch about them putting it back on again) and any 'miracle' health cure which has absolutely no basis in scientific fact (preferably involving vegetables or the waving of crystals). It also sports a collection of cartoons (never the same since they dropped Schulz's *Peanuts*). A *Daily Mail* reader is probably the most likely to contribute to a radio phone-in while being in possession of a quarter of the facts. Some cruelly claim that the easiest way to confuse a *Daily Mail* reader is to tell them that paedophiles are the natural prey of asylum seekers.*

---

* Generate your own amusing *Mail* headlines at http://www. qwghlm.co.uk/toys/dailymail

On balance, though, the *Mail* is probably nothing like as reactionary as its detractors would like to claim, and *Mail*-bashing is a cheap and easy sport.

The *Daily Telegraph*

Standing alone against the UK's drift to the centre-left, like the last soldier who does not know the war is over, the *Telegraph* was, in the dark days of William Hague and Iain Duncan Smith, the only paper to give its support to the beleaguered and increasingly out-of-touch Conservative party; it was amusing to see the hoops it had to jump through on a daily basis in order to keep this support alive. However, as Tory policies once again begin to chime with Worcester Woman and Essex Man, it's amusing to speculate that the grand old *Telegraph* may yet have the last laugh.

It's undeniably a serious paper, giving column inches to weighty issues and having scant regard for the tawdrier end of popular culture. It has boasted among its writers the Fleet Street grandee W.F. Deedes, the Canadian conservative Mark Steyn and education experts such as John Clare and Chris Woodhead. But it has started, in recent years, to dally with *Mail*-style celebrity obsession, which has earned it the nickname the 'Tottygraph' from *Private Eye*. And it exists in a strange world where half a page is given over to the ailments of pets called Bunty and Flippy, and where one could be forgiven for thinking nobody attends state school, nobody has a home worth less than £300,000 and nobody comes from the north. And nobody, perish the thought, votes Labour. (One is irresistibly reminded of what was possibly Neil Kinnock's best speech, a warning about life in Tory Britain: 'I warn you not to be ordinary, I warn you not to be young, I

warn you not to fall ill, and I warn you not to grow old.')
A few once dallied with the Liberal Democrats but were
brought back to the fold by those nice clean-cut boys
David Cameron and George Osborne.

Interestingly, though, a 2004 MORI poll indicated
that only two-thirds of *Telegraph* readers supported the
Conservative party, with 15 per cent Labour and 17
per cent Liberal Democrat.[*] One has to assume that a
large proportion of the Labour-voting *Telegraph* readership either takes the paper for comedy purposes, or are
activists living in deep *Spooks*-style cover in English country villages in order to subvert the enemy from within.
(In contrast, only 5 per cent of *Guardian* readers vote
Conservative, which one can easily write off as madness
or research.)

> *Public opinion is a compound of folly, weakness, preju-
> dice, wrong feeling, right feeling, obstinacy, and newspaper
> paragraphs.*
>
> Sir Robert Peel (prime minister 1834–35 and
> 1841–46)

Politicians' worst media moments

It's not surprising that the advice given to today's politicians is to err on the side of caution, treat every
microphone as if it's a live one, and always remember
– someone, somewhere is watching. Let us take a look at
some of those occasions when our politicians were not
'on-message' – and perhaps revealed a little too many of
their human foibles.

---

[*] Ipsos-MORI poll, 'Voting by Readership', July–December 2004.

Sing-along-a-Redwood: At the time John Redwood was a pretty unpopular secretary of state for Wales, and he is increasingly irritated these days to see the clip replayed of the time in 1993 when he very obviously didn't know the words to the Welsh national anthem. Like someone in church suddenly confronted with one of those 'modern hymns' with the awkward tunes, John bobbed his head from side to side and mouthed something which he hoped resembled the noises which were coming from the people around him. Sadly for him, the cameras' close-up revealed it all. The BBC got into trouble in 2007 for running a story about a totally unrelated issue and illustrating it with the aforementioned clip. Redwood's successor William Hague fared rather better, having been taught the words by his Welsh wife Ffion. **Cringe factor: 7/10**

Sing-along-a-Lilley: It was again the turn of the Conservative party to cringe in their seats when, in 1998, their deputy leader Peter Lilley performed his own version of 'Land of Hope and Glory', changing the words to 'Land of Chattering Classes'. The fact that his singing voice was, shall we say, not exactly of Pavarotti standard just added to the pain. **Cringe factor: 6/10**

Perspiring to greatness: 'Don't sweat the small stuff' is advice often given by the good and the great to those starting out. But at the 2000 Labour party conference, the last one available to get things right before the stern test of a general election, Tony Blair visibly found his Sure for Men letting him down. The spin doctors went into overdrive: would this put the voters off? Would it be a case of 'Things Can Only Get Sweatier'?

One was irresistibly reminded of the televised US debate two decades earlier between Nixon and Kennedy, the former sweating and riled, the latter relaxed and calm. And it happened again in 2006 – mired in the cash-for-peerages scandal and beset with questions about his departure, Blair's speech on the NHS saw him looking shinier and damper than a Glastonbury tent. To be fair, though, how many people could do the job of prime minister and remain cool under the heat of press and public scrutiny? (Those who have met Bill Clinton say he is always astonishingly fragrant – maybe US presidents have access to some secret anti-stress formula developed in Area 51.) **Cringe factor: 7/10**

Bombing Russia: So, Ronald Reagan – the man who said with a straight face that there could be a 'limited nuclear war in Europe'. He believed literally in the biblical prophecy of Armageddon and cheerfully asserted, during his 1984 re-election campaign, that our generation could be the one to see it. Not surprising that many of us just wanted to hide under our duvets with a can of spam and listen to Frankie Goes To Hollywood.

But his best-known gaffe is perhaps the one which sealed many people's opinion of him for all time as a dangerous warmonger. On live radio in 1984, supposedly intending it to be a quip and thinking himself off-air, Reagan declared: 'My fellow Americans, I'm pleased to tell you today that I've signed legislation that will outlaw Russia forever. We begin bombing in five minutes.' So that's what you get, people said, for putting an actor in the White House. We can laugh now, but at the time this seemed as bad, as frightening, as stupid and as cringeworthy as an American president could possibly get. Which just goes to prove Karl Marx's aphorism that history repeats itself, first as tragedy and then as farce. **Cringe factor: 10/10**

Don't thump the voters: To the delight of the viewing public, the moribund 2001 election campaign briefly came to life when, on camera, protestor Craig Evans hurled an egg at then deputy prime minister John Prescott, and the political bruiser retaliated in kind with a powerful left hook. 'Two Jabs' headlines inevitably followed. 'John is John,' said Tony Blair gnomically, refusing to comment further. Although interviewed by police, Prescott was not charged with any offence, the Crown Prosecution Service taking the line that Prescott had acted in self-defence. Craig Evans, although held for a short while in police custody, was not charged. He was perhaps lucky – in these post-9/11, security-conscious days, he could have found himself getting a spell in Guantanamo Bay. **Cringe factor: 7/10**

George and the 'asshole': While seeking election in 2000, towering intellectual and campaigner for world peace George W. Bush caught sight of a *New York Times* reporter he didn't especially like in the crowd. Dubya muttered to running-mate Dick Cheney that the reporter, Adam Clymer, was a 'major-league asshole', to which Cheney responded: 'Yeah, big-time.' All caught on camera and microphone. **Cringe factor: 7/10**

'Yo, Blair': Again, a George Dubya Bush slip-up while thinking he was not being overheard (and let's pause, for a moment, to ponder on the thought processes of a Presidentialist of the Unified Stetsons who thought *nobody* would be listening in on him during a G8 summit). His famously 'matey/folksy' but also superior-sounding greeting to the British prime minister has, for some, come to epitomise the relationship between the two men. It was supposedly a bantering and respectful friendship between equals, but actually seems to have been a case of George inviting Tony to jump and Tony grinning and asking George how high, before they go off to pray together and compare toothpaste. **Cringe factor: 6/10**

Life's a beach: Labour leader Neil Kinnock started his reign with a little walk on Brighton beach for the media with wife Glenys in 1983. All well and good, until he tripped and fell at the water's edge, getting a good soaking and giving TV folks a classic piece of footage to replay at each subsequent Kinnock 'stumble'.

However, it doesn't end there. Twenty-four years after his tumble in front of the cameras, the now Lord Kinnock took another wander down to Brighton beach. This time, he received a four-letter barracking from the pensioners described later as 'semi-clad' who were protesting there about the government's ineptitude over pension schemes. Gritting his teeth afterwards, Lord Kinnock asserted that the protestors were 'very decent people' and had been 'dreadfully let down by the system'. **Cringe factor: 8/10**

Jacques Chirac, master of the *entente cordiale*: In 2005, before Jamie Oliver had started to pull apart school dinners, another critic of the British menu came bounding on to the scene – France's President Chirac, who remarked in what he thought was a private chat with

Russian president Vladimir Putin and German chancellor Gerhard Schroeder: 'The only thing that [the
British] have ever done for European agriculture is mad
cow disease … You cannot trust people who have such
bad cuisine.'* This was said while waiting for the decision
on which city would host the 2012 Olympics, so maybe
Jacques went for some fish and chips afterwards to cheer
up. Or some vintage wine, made with sour grapes. **Cringe
factor: 6/10**

The pick-it line: In 2007, Gordon Brown was seen briefly
excavating his nose while sitting on the front bench of
the House of Commons behind Tony Blair. A nation
baulked at the future PM's antics, and they gave the tab-
loids a whole new load of 'bogeyman' insults to pile on
top of the 'Stalinist' jibes. **Cringe factor: 9/10**

Don't cross the Mersey: The ever-diplomatic Boris
Johnson, the man who now runs London, and who has
said that his 'chances of being PM are about as good as
the chances of finding Elvis on Mars, or my being rein-
carnated as an olive'. An entire cornucopia of entertaining gaffes and howlers to choose from, but somehow
the one that sticks most in people's minds is the one for
which he was forced to wear sackcloth. Yes, the infamous
Spectator article in which Boris accused the city of 'wallow-
ing in its victim status'.† He should have known that hell
hath no fury like a Scouser scorned, and within the week
his leader Michael Howard had packed the wild-haired
shadow culture secretary on the train up north – off to
the land of Brookside, the Albert Dock and the Cavern

* Quoted by Robert Barr, Associated Press, 5 July 2005.
† *Spectator*, unsigned leader, 16 October 2004.

Club to apologise in person. And apologise he did. Never was there a man more penitent. Radio stations, TV studios, local papers – all were collared for Boris's penance as he tried to pour oil on a troubled Mersey. It seemed to do little good. 'I think coming here makes things worse. It's not the right response at all', said Mike Storey, leader of the city council. A few years later, Boris was trying again to build bridges, this time by being part of the team giving political support to Liverpool during its 2008 tenure as European Capital of Culture. **Cringe factor: 7/10**

On the record: the hands of history

It's true, then, that what is said or done off the record can get politicians into a lot of trouble. But sometimes, they just make it all too easy for us – through simply saying what they have intended us to hear.

Some famous utterances and their full context should give us some idea of how, perhaps, politicians do not always go down in history in the way they intend.

'The lady's not for turning.' (Margaret Thatcher, 1980)
At the party conference in Brighton in October 1980, Mrs Thatcher confronted those who doubted her economic policies. She cemented her reputation as someone who was not likely to change her mind by telling those who were looking out for the famous 'U-Turn': 'You turn if you want to. The lady's not for turning!' She got the expected round of applause, although it unfortunately came halfway through the punch line. In years to come, even her detractors would come to say that they admired her single-mindedness; unfortunately, her unwillingness to compromise may just have been what brought her down.

'I feel the hand of history on our shoulder.'
(Tony Blair, 1998)

In April 1998, arriving in Belfast for the process of trying to come to a resolution for Northern Ireland, Tony
Blair famously faced the cameras – and gave probably the
best illustration of someone trying to make a rehearsed
remark seem off-the-cuff. Aware of the possible momen-
tousness of the occasion, Blair told the world that today
was 'not a day for soundbites', and promptly gave one:
'I feel the hand of history on our shoulder in respect to
this. I really do. I just think we need to acknowledge that
and respond to it.' In retrospect, the 'I really do' seems
to undermine the comment rather than give it greater
weight. Of course, the Northern Ireland peace deal is
one of the achievements for which even Blair's enemies
give him grudging credit these days, even after some
thought at the time that he'd been given the inverted
two fingers of history.

'He got on his bike and looked for work.'
(Norman Tebbit, 1981)

Famously misquoted as 'on your bike', Norman Tebbit's
exhortation to the unemployed rioters of Britain to go
out and seek jobs which were not there was, even at
the time, seen as a little misdirected. Citing his father's
proactive attitude towards employment during the 1930s
was all well and good, but at the same time no doubt
rather offensive to those millions of people up and down
the country who *were* getting on their bikes and finding
the Job Centre boards bare.

'Go back to your constituencies and prepare for government.' (David Steel, 1981)

Liberal party leader David Steel's optimistic exhortation to his troops in 1981 is symbolic of the eternal problem faced by the third biggest party in British politics. Some argue that they offer a credible alternative, freed from the shackles of the old 'left' and 'right' definitions. ('The only fresh thing on the menu', ran the SDP-Liberal Alliance's slogan in 1983, under which, on one billboard, some wag had scrawled: 'Sell by 9th June.') Others deride them as irrelevant and argue that politics would be better off without them – that people would have a clearer choice under a two-party system. To a political outsider, this latter view seems demented.

Amusingly, Nick Clegg appeared to be channelling Steel at the 2008 Liberal Democrat conference, when he announced to delegates that they were 'heading for government'. (Maybe he meant local?)

'Our enemies are innovative and resourceful, and so are we. They never stop thinking about new ways to harm our country and our people, and neither do we.' (George W. Bush, 1994)

This sort of thing is just a gift to the 9/11 conspiracy theorists, said the commentators. 'Stop it, George!' they pleaded. At least in retirement he will have less opportunity to be gaffe-prone, one hopes.

'Anybody who enjoys being in the House of Commons probably needs psychiatric help.' (Ken Livingstone)

This, one imagines, is why Ken found other routes into politics. He also said that 'if voting changed anything, they'd abolish it'. One could point out that it changed the mayor of London.

Youth versus age

Another aspect of today's media dominance of politics is the obsession with our politicians' ages. They are, after all, celebrities of a sort, and no celebrity is mentioned in the papers without their age being given afterwards like a talisman. It seems politicians cannot win – if they are too young (under 45) they are lambasted for their lack of experience, while if they are too old (over 60, usually) they are castigated for being ancient warhorses out of touch with modern times. Is there a happy medium?

- Tony Blair, who won an election four days before turning 44, was the youngest prime minister since Robert Banks Jenkinson, Earl of Liverpool, who took office in 1791 the day after his 42nd birthday. Blair was the youngest post-war prime minister, although David Cameron, born in 1966, may yet beat that record, depending on when the election is held … and if he wins, of course.

- William Gladstone, who retired from his second term in 1894 at the age of 84, holds the record as the oldest serving prime minister. Winston Churchill is the second oldest, having resigned in 1955 at the age of 81.

- If the Conservative party gains power in 2010 and George Osborne remains as chancellor (at the age of 38 or 39) he will be the youngest man to have occupied that position since Randolph Churchill held the post in 1886 at the age of 37.

- At the age of 36, William Hague became the youngest leader of the Conservative party since Pitt the Younger 200 years earlier. He surrounded himself with wise old heads, though, and seems to be maturing into one of his party's elder statesmen himself these days.

- Jo Swinson, the Liberal Democrat MP for East Dunbartonshire, born on 5 February 1980, is the youngest MP of the 2005 Parliament. The youngest MP is traditionally known as the 'Baby of the House'.

- Another Liberal Democrat, Matthew Taylor, held the Baby of the House title for ten years (1987–97).

- Party leaders William Hague, Tony Blair and Charles Kennedy all started their political lives as the youngest MP in their party.

- The 'Father of the House' is not necessarily the oldest MP, but the one who has served for the longest unbroken period. Labour's Alan Williams, MP for Swansea West, became Father of the House in 2005, having held the seat since 1964.

- 66-year-old Sir Menzies 'Ming' Campbell resigned as leader of the Liberal Democrats after continual media suggestion that his age made him unsuitable for the job. 'They say age is going to be an issue at the next election – of course it is, I'm going to make it one', Sir Menzies had asserted at his 2007 conference speech. Just a few months later, across the Atlantic, Senator John McCain was selected as the Republican candidate for the US presidency at the age of 71. As our American friends would no doubt say: 'Go figure.'

- In 2007, eighteen-year-old A Level student William Lloyd became Britain's youngest councillor after winning in Brentwood, Essex.

- The narrative of the 2008 US presidential election was driven to an extent by the obsession with Senator John McCain's age and the fact that, at the end of a four-year term, he'd be 76, the oldest president for some time – the Republicans, aware of this, developed a strategy for portraying him as old and wise, rather than old and decrepit. To an extent, it worked – especially when younger running-mate Sarah Palin was thrown into the mix. Although he didn't win, of course.

Talk to me!

Voters often complain that politicians don't actually want to come and discuss the issues that matter – that they don't want to pop round and debate on the doorstep, put leaflets through the door and so on. When Liberal Democrat leader Nick Clegg announced in 2008 that, post-conference, he was going to be phoning a few thousand people up for a chat, maybe a good many voters rubbed their hands with glee, relishing the chance to have a productive and meaningful debate with a major party leader, or at least give him a multiple choice quiz. 'Hi, Nick, great to hear from you. For one hundred pounds, how much is the weekly pension? a) £30, b) £60, c) £90 or d) £120? No guessing, now. This is the kind of stuff you're meant to *know*.' Disappointingly, the communication turned out to be just a recorded message. 'Hi there! Con-*grad*-ulations! This is Nick Clegg of the Liberal Democrats! Listen to this message and you could win a free weekend discussing Proportional Representation with Lynne Featherstone in Brighton.' One is not sure how he was talked into this – maybe he said he was going to phone up 'more than 30' people and then tried to backtrack by saying he'd exaggerated a bit.

Being fair, though, there are an awful lot of voters and not many people available to get round them all. Those who put in the legwork for political parties are frustrated by the misconceptions. Labour Haringey councillor Emma Jones expresses these frustrations forcefully:

> Leaflets are delivered entirely by volunteers, and find-ing fit and able volunteers who can give up the time (particularly in areas which are predominantly one party or another) is often very difficult indeed – most of our party members are either older people who can-not walk far, or younger people who are extremely busy with jobs and family lives. I think the public thinks that leaflets are delivered by paid staff.

The Green party's Caroline Lucas, in the run-up to her election as leader, pointed out that the lack of state fund-ing for political parties means that politics means raising money, and that disadvantages the smaller parties:

> Scandalously in the UK, political activity comes at a price. If elected [as Green party leader] I'm deter-mined that we field a record number of candidates in the next general election.[*]

Blogger Iain Dale asserts that voters aren't always neces-sarily clear what they want, either:

---

* 'You Ask The Questions: Caroline Lucas', *Independent*, 11 August 2008.

I get sick and tired of people who on the one hand
want clear blue water between the parties and then ask
plaintively, why can't you all agree? You can't please all
of the people all of the time in politics and it's about
time politicians got used to the fact.

What about talking politics in general? The Hansard
Society's latest *Audit of Political Engagement*, based on a
representative sample of 1,073 adults over eighteen,
found that only two in five British people had 'discussed
politics or political news with family or friends' in the
last two to three years. The same survey found that a dis-
appointing 52–53 per cent of people were 'absolutely
certain to vote'. However, the previous year's audit had
asked very different questions – had people discussed
unemployment? Taxes? The economy? Crime? Of course
they had – these are the issues which matter to people,
and which are talked about in pubs and on buses up and
down the country.[*]

But the respondents in 2008 didn't necessarily equate
the fact that they discussed these issues with an interest
in 'politics'. After all, what is politics? A bunch of stuffed
shirts arguing at each other in the Houses of Parliament?
A lot of venal, self-serving creeps who, if they are not fid-
dling their expenses, are sneaking off for trysts with their
researchers and secretaries in their hugely extended
lunch hours and their obscenely long summer holidays?
These are the stereotyped ideas which prevent people
who are genuinely interested, motivated and enthusias-
tic about changing the country from getting involved in

---

[*] *Hansard Audits of Political Engagement*, 2008, 2007: http://
hansardsociety.org.uk/blogs/parliament_and_government/pages/
Audit-of-Political-Engagement.aspx

politics – they see politics as a barrier, rather than a tool for change.

How often have you heard politicians saying that they want less concentration on their own lives, on the 'Westminster village', on gossip and tittle-tattle, and more on the issues which matter to people? How many times have we heard politicians in government saying they want to be left to 'get on with it'?

Maybe voters are frustrated with what they see as a nebulous approach to these very difficult issues – perhaps because we, slightly unreasonably, expect straight answers to pretty wobbly questions. Like these:

Can I get a decent school for my children? Education, education, education? Or just crowd control? In these days of scaremongering, parents could be forgiven for thinking their child will turn into a knife-wielding ASBO thug with tattoos and poor diction if they don't start them off in the 'right' school from day one. Parental 'choice', one of the biggest misnomers of the last twenty years, now accounts for a lot of heartache in the school system. Parents will, it seems, do anything to elbow their way into their desired school, especially if there is one nearby which is perceived as much 'better' than the one on their doorstep.

Have I got a good hospital nearby? And am I likely to come out with MRSA or something else which means I'm worse off than when I went in?

Why have they stopped my local bus service? The usual answer given for this is that not enough people were using it. It's the kind of thing where there is a 'consultation' period, which means a superficial attempt to let you know what they're going to be doing before they do it, and a very narrow window of time in which to complain and gather evidence for your case. Use this window well and wisely.

Why is my local Post Office being closed? Apparently they have to make money, and allegedly it's good enough that you have one half a mile away that you should be able to use. The fact that it's more like a mile away, up a hill and not on any regular public transport route will of course not make any difference to your rheumatic 83-year-old neighbour when she goes to collect her pension.

Is it safe for me to walk the streets at night? And should surveillance bother me if I have 'nothing to hide'? Here I can do no better than refer you to the excellent *Surveillance Unlimited: How We've Become the Most Watched People on Earth* by Keith Laidler (Icon, 2008). Read it and you will never look at your average suburban street in quite the same way again. If CCTV really does develop along the lines suggested, with enhancement programs and high definition, then one suspects the cameras will be strangely adept at capturing every pixel of minor motoring offences and yet oddly deficient when it comes to displaying the faces of thugs who have robbed people in broad daylight.

The power of the pressure group

- Campaigners for fathers' rights group Fathers 4 Justice have given the government a few surprises in recent years. In 2004, two 'powder missiles' laden with bluish-purple cornflour were lobbed at Tony Blair in the Commons by members of the group. The public gallery is screened off from the Commons by a glass shield, but the flour-lobbers had managed to gain access to an open area by being guests of former Labour MP Baroness Golding.

- In the summer of 2008, protestors from the same group twice scaled the roof of the London home of deputy Labour leader Harriet Harman.

- In February 2003, one of the UK's biggest ever demonstrations took place against the Iraq war. (Groups formed to oppose a particular issue like the Iraq war are sometimes known as 'fire brigades'.) One gets the usual variation in estimates of attendance at these things – 16 million if you believe the organisers, or 26 plus a dog if you believe the police. Those aren't the exact numbers, but they may as well be. Noted for one of the best demo slogans of all time: 'Make Tea, Not War.' The vocal opposition to the war at the demonstration included contributions from the Lib Dems' Charles Kennedy, playwright Harold Pinter (who disappointingly didn't deliver an enigmatic speech full of pauses) and the former US presidential wannabe Jesse Jackson. It made no difference – US and UK forces steamed into Iraq the following month.

- There are plenty of others to choose from. Greenpeace, the old favourite of the environmental activist movement, now has both a website and a blog (see bibliography). The Taxpayers' Alliance campaigns for lower taxes. I Want A Referendum does what it says on the tin, campaigning for the referendum on the EU

Constitution, promised by the government in 2005, to materialise. No2ID makes clear its vocal opposition to the proposed identity card system. And there are many, many more. Choose your cause carefully, and be prepared to end up fighting against faceless bureaucracy, political indifference and, at times, public misunderstanding.

Lobbying your MP

If there's an issue you feel strongly about, attempt to engage your MP's support. Here are a few tips for doing this effectively:

- Stick to one issue per email/letter. If you have a lot to get off your chest you may be tempted to put it all in, but this will just sound like unfocused rambling.

- Provide some evidence to support your view – statistics, facts, references to newspaper articles and websites or photographs.

- Be clear what you are asking the MP to do: write in response, clarify the government's standpoint, write a letter to the relevant minister or something else.

- If you feel very strongly about a particular issue, don't write to the relevant minister – write to your MP. Because if your local school is threatened with closure and you write to the education secretary, or you want to complain about your hospital and you write to the health secretary, then the chances are that he or she will never even see your letter, and all you will get in return is a printed-out policy statement attached to a letter written by a minion. But if you write to your MP, he or she must write on your behalf to the minister responsible and should get a proper written response. It takes longer, but it might just make more of an impact.

• If you want to discuss something with your MP in person, you can arrange to meet them, either on your own or with a group of like-minded people. You can do this by writing to them and arranging to meet at the House of Commons, or by going along to one of their consultation sessions or 'surgeries'. These will be held in church halls, libraries and similar places in their constituency, usually at weekends, and should be well advertised. Try looking on your MP's website, if he or she has one, (MPs' websites are listed at http://www.parliament.uk/directories/hciolists/alms.cfm) and, again, be sure you know what you want from the meeting and be ready to explain your views clearly. Be firm, but polite.

PolFax: Big Issues

14–1: ratio of British citizens to CCTV cameras, as claimed by former shadow home secretary David Davis[*]

4.2 million: number of security cameras in the UK, as claimed by a 2002 study by academics Michael McCahill and Clive Norris[†]

1 in 8: proportion of British children to have had a gadget (mobile phone, iPod etc.) stolen in the last three years[‡]

[*] BBC News, http://news.bbc.co.uk/1/hi/uk/7451552.stm
[†] *Guardian*, 20 June 2006.
[‡] Home Secretary Jacqui Smith, quoted in *Daily Mail*, 15 May 2008.

40,000: number of people interviewed over twelve months for the British Crime Survey. Home Secretary Jacqui Smith announced in 2007 that the survey would include children for the first time[*]

56: percentage of British people who believe immigrants get a 'better deal' when it comes to allocation of public services[†]

6 billion: journeys made by bus, coach or rail each year in the UK[‡]

8–13: percentage of eighteen- and nineteen-year-olds pursuing a higher education course in the three constituencies where take-up is lowest – Nottingham North, Sheffield Brightside and Bristol South (compared with 33 per cent nationally)[§]

53: in 2008, percentage of Oxford undergraduates who attended state schools[¶]

---

[*] Research Development Statistics British Crime Survey: http://www.homeoffice.gov.uk/rds/bcs1.html
[†] MORI poll, January 2007.
[‡] Department for Transport figures: http://www.dft.gov.uk/press/releases/pressarchive/tacklingcrimeonpublictransport
[§] Peter Gates, Sarah Coward and Tina Byrom, 'Young Participation in Higher Education in the Constituency of Nottingham North', University of Nottingham, 2007.
[¶] Polly Curtis, 'Oxford and Cambridge fail to improve state school intake', *Guardian*, 18 February 2008.

Vox Pops

If you make the most of [education], you study hard, you do your homework, and you make an effort to be smart, you can do well. If you don't, you get stuck in Iraq.

John Kerry, former US presidential candidate,
not exactly winning over the Forces voters

It's no exaggeration to say that the undecideds could go one way or another.

And the intellectual giant who beat him –
George W. Bush, US president, 2001–09

7

The Round-up

I never vote for anyone. I always vote against.
W.C. Fields, actor (1880–1946)

Frequently Asked Questions

Q. *So I really ought to bother to vote, then?*
A1. It's up to you. Yes, you may say that it's a farce, that politicians are so disengaged from the people that they don't listen to what we say anyway, and that the democratic voice of the people has been reduced to the absolute minimum necessary to call the United Kingdom a democracy. But if you sit at home and do nothing, it's very unlikely that anything is going to change for the better.
A2. Nobody can force you. If you don't, though, then you haven't really got a leg to stand on if you then moan about the state of the country. And remember people have died for the right to vote.

Q. *Could I ever be made to vote?*
A. Compulsory voting is an option which has been considered at various times. It came to the fore at the September 2007 Democracy Day held by the Fabian Society, at which speaker Fiona MacTaggart claimed: 'We are trying to educate people about voting through citizenship classes and raising awareness of the importance of voting. As far as I can see, the compulsory vote would address any problems

of laziness.'* The voter, according to this argument, is the problem. Perhaps a more powerful argument is that politics should be made to engage with people, to raise the profile of the agenda to the point where people realise it affects every nuance of their lives, and where they take a conscious, meaningful decision to vote. After all, is an uninformed compulsory vote – one where it is merely another civic duty, like paying taxes – actually a meaningful vote? 32 countries worldwide have compulsory voting, of which the following enforce it: Argentina, Australia, Belgium, Brazil, Chile, Cyprus, Democratic Republic of the Congo, Ecuador, Fiji, Lebanon, Liechtenstein, Nauru, Peru, Singapore, Switzerland (in the canton of Schaffhausen only), Turkey and Uruguay. The argument was made by the Institute for Public Policy Research in 2006 that 'compulsory turnout is not compulsory voting. Ballot papers can be spoiled or can contain options to vote for "none of the above"'.†

Q. *Why don't I get leaflets through the door from every candidate?*

A. They cannot possibly cover every base. They can't afford to, for one thing. Parties have limited resources and it just doesn't make sense to canvass and leaflet every voter in every constituency, much as they'd like to. And leaflets are delivered by volunteers. There is an assumption that the voter will make some effort to find out who is standing in their constituency and which of the candidates has the views closest to theirs.

---

* Quoted at http://www.opendemocracy.net/ourkingdom/articles/
for-compulsory-voting
† Ben Rogers, assistant director of IPPR, quoted in 'Only
compulsory turnout can restore principle of universal suffrage', at
http://www.ippr.org.uk/pressreleases/?id=2083

Q. *Shouldn't they make the effort, though?*
A. From outside, it might seem as if every party has the resources to do so, but that just isn't true. Leaflets and newsletters are delivered by volunteers, who all have other responsibilities to fit in around their political activities. Asking this question puts the onus on the party rather than on you, the voter, to be an active and concerned citizen. If there are issues about which you feel passionate, you won't wait for a leaflet to come through the door before you do anything about them.

Q. *So why do they bother putting anyone up if they're not going to fight the seat?*
A. Often, a candidate knows full well they have no chance of winning and is there a) as a repository for the votes of that party's supporters in the constituency who would otherwise be aggrieved at having nowhere to place their cross, and b) because, frankly, it looks bad for a major party not to put up candidates. In theory, it also enables the party's manifesto and policies to be debated at hustings and discussed in every constituency. Whether that particular party has a chance of winning or not is not really the issue – it's good for democracy for voters to have as wide a choice as possible.

Q. *Do they sometimes fight seats knowing they're going to lose?*
A. Would-be MPs often fight hopeless seats as a baptism of fire. Tony Blair first fought the seat of Beaconsfield and lost his deposit, but his campaign brought him to the attention of the leadership; former Tory leader Michael Howard, before his comfortable win in Folkestone in 1983, had twice fought and lost the safe Labour seat of Edge Hill in Liverpool. Of course, you can't *look* as if you

know you're going to lose, as you'd end up doing even more badly and as if you can't run a decent campaign. And at the back of every MP's mind will be those occasions on which the supposedly safe seat has fallen, giving one party or another a kick in the teeth.

Q. *So if I'm not in a marginal constituency, I'll never get anyone coming and asking for my vote, then?*
A. That's the cynical view, which may be right. Perhaps if there is a sea change in the next couple of general elections – fewer diehards and more grave-turners, maybe – then we may see a subtle change in this approach. But don't forget there will be other ways in which the candidates will make themselves available – expect to see them popping up on local radio and TV, for example, which are often better ways of getting their message across than 'doorstepping'.

Q. *And when someone comes round and says: 'May I ask how you intend to vote?', I can say: 'I'm going to put a cross in the box next to the name of my preferred candidate.'*
A. Yes. They'll have heard that one.

Q. *Right. Do you **have** to mark your ballot paper with an X?*
A. What you have to do is give a 'clear indication' of your intention. As long as your mark in the box next to the name of your preferred candidate is unambiguous, it can be a cross, a tick or even a little smiley face.

Q. *What if I make a mistake on the ballot paper?*
A. If you spoil a ballot paper *by accident*, ask the presiding officer for another one, and don't put the spoilt ballot paper in the ballot box. You'll be given a new paper and

your spoilt paper will be put in an envelope and sealed. It may be scrutinised later during the count.

Q. *Could abstaining be dangerous? Could it let in the bunch I don't want?*

A. Here's a scare story which was effectively blown out of the water. In the 2005 election campaign, Labour tried to claim that, if one in ten Labour voters were to abstain, that would hand a majority to Michael Howard's Conservatives. It's a measure of how frightened they were, post-Iraq, that they might actually lose. The assumption was based on the dual statistical fallacy that a) all the non-voters would be concentrated in the 150-odd marginal constituencies where a Labour–Tory battle might make a difference, and b) in other seats, the key Labour vote would come out much as before. Pollsters MORI called this a 'simplification of reality', while conceding that Labour might well have had a problem with tactical voting after Iraq. In the event, a Labour government was returned for the third time in a row, albeit with Tony Blair's majority slashed by over 100 – that such an unpopular government could be returned to power at all was an indictment, some said, of an unappealing and weak opposition. And yes, they could have been right.

Q. *Who are Worcester Woman and Essex Man? Why should I care?*

A. 'Worcester Woman' is a name given to a particular kind of voter, seen as white-collar and interested in issues that affect quality of life. The term first came to public prominence in the 1997 election, as it was thought voters from this tranche of society had been largely responsible for sweeping Tony Blair to power – Worcester Woman is seen as equally likely to be able to swing back again to the Conservatives. 'Essex Man' epitomises the self-made working-class man with right-wing tendencies – and was seen as the ideal Thatcherite voter. In the 1980s he'd have driven a Mondeo, so these days is more likely to be seen in a 4×4. He has little tolerance for immigration or liberal approaches to crime, and may own a former council property in suburbia. Don't discount such broad and probably insulting stereotypes – they help inform the thinking on which many policies are formulated.

Q. *So how do I get more involved in politics?*
A. One very easy way is join at 'grass roots' – get involved with a local campaign like one to save a post office or school threatened with closure, or a local community forum. Plenty of people end up doing this without even thinking of themselves as 'politically' active. There are demonstrations to go on, petitions to sign. Then there's the parish council and the local council. Lobby your councillor and/or MP on matters close to your heart. And vote, of course. Always, always vote. If you want to become an active member of one of the political parties, just contact your local branch and ask what you can do. They'll be only too happy to have you on board.

Q. *Does power corrupt?*
A. It's usually true that people go into politics with honest intentions. It's also often true that people often end up compromising their values in order to hang on to power. Even then, this can be borne out of honourable motivations – to compromise on one issue in order to be in a position to get other things done. There is no doubt that some high-profile stories have given the public an

impression of untrustworthiness, but generally we have no reason to disbelieve politicians who say they genuinely want to work for our benefit. It's not hopelessly naïve, provided we exercise our duty as citizens and pin them down, make them justify themselves and constantly ask them to back up their rhetoric with action.

Q. *Can I trust anything they say?*
A. As we have seen, politicians will often be in the position of having to give the most suitable answer for their party at that particular time. They may not be lying, exactly – just being very careful not to give out information which could be inaccurate or could get them into a lot of trouble. It is our role as voters to hold them to account, and to make sure they do the things they said they were going to do.

Here are some suggestions for listening to what politicians say, and imagining how they might be different with just a subtle tweak in the subject of the sentence.

Irregularities: Political 'irregular verbs'

I have joined the party which is true to my beliefs.
You are a floor-crosser.
(He is a filthy treacherous swine.)

I am a person of strong convictions.
You are unswaying.
(He is a stubborn old goat.)

I have decided to spend more time with my family.
You are stepping down.
(He is jumping before he is pushed.)

I am confronting the minister with the unpalatable truth.
You are asking awkward questions.
(He is a right royal pain in the neck.)

I am an excellent advocate for what I believe in.
You are quite zealous when you get worked up.
(He is a monomaniac.)

I believe that the prime minister is the person to lead us through the current crisis.
You are to be admired for standing by the prime minister in troubled times.
(He is the last rat to leave the sinking ship.)

Some Random Trivia

- John Major's famous 'soapbox' from the 1992 general election, which first came out as he campaigned in Luton (or possibly Cheltenham – sources vary), was described by some as an orange crate, but was actually a document box from Conservative central office. It was tested for strength and suitability by Special Branch and was reinforced with tape so that he didn't fall through it (which would have made for a *You've Been Framed* moment to rival Neil Kinnock on the beach). Its re-emergence in 1997 did not go down quite so well; this time, he was heckled by students chanting: 'You'll be on the dole, John.'

- Both Tony Blair and Gordon Brown made their maiden speeches in the House of Commons in July 1983 – Tony on the 6th, Gordon on the 27th.

- Mrs Thatcher's office once suggested to Buckingham Palace that the prime minister and the Queen should coordinate outfits at official functions. The palace's excellent and somewhat frosty reply was that this was not necessary, as Her Majesty did not notice what Mrs Thatcher was wearing anyway.

- For two years in the mid-1970s, the United States of America was led for the only time by a man who had been elected neither president nor vice-president. After the resignation of Nixon in 1974, Gerald Ford took over – and Ford himself had stepped in as vice-president after the resignation of Spiro T. Agnew over financial irregularities in 1973. As president, he appointed the similarly unelected Nelson Rockefeller as his deputy.

- In 2007, the *Daily Telegraph* chose its Top 100 most influential people on the Left and on the Right. The only person to appear in the Top Ten of both lists was Tony Blair (at number two and number ten respectively).*

- Benjamin Disraeli's maiden speech did not go well, and hecklers eventually forced him to stop – with the prophetic words: 'Though I sit down now, the time will come when you will hear me.'

- In May 2007 a Conservative district council candidate, Shirley Bowes, standing for election to the council in Sedgefield (Tony Blair's political stamping ground, of course), did not receive a single vote. Shirley was not even allowed to vote for herself because she lived

---

* *Daily Telegraph*, 'Most Influential Right-Wingers in UK' and 'The Left List', 23 April 2008.

outside the ward, which was won by Labour's Lucy Hovells with 441 votes. One wonders what happened to the fifteen people who must have signed Shirley's nomination papers.

PolFax: Top Ten Best Prime Ministerial Nicknames

- Arthur Wellesley, Duke of Wellington: 'The Iron Duke'; 'Saviour of the Nations'

- Viscount Palmerston: 'Lord Cupid'; 'Lord Pumicestone'

- Arthur Balfour: 'Bloody Balfour'

- David Lloyd George: 'The Welsh Wizard'

- Winston Churchill: 'Winnie'

- Harold Macmillan: 'Supermac'; 'Mac the Knife'

- James Callaghan: 'Sunny Jim'

- Margaret Thatcher: 'Milk Snatcher' (as education secretary); 'The Iron Lady' (as PM)

- John Major: 'The Grey Man'; 'Honest John'

- Tony Blair: 'Teflon Tony'; 'Phoney Tony'

- Gordon Brown: 'McBroon'; 'Mr Bean'; 'Bottler Brown'

The Numbers Game: Total turnout at the last ten UK general elections

Year	Percentage
1970	72.0
1974 (February)	78.8
1974 (October)	72.8
1979	76.0
1983	72.7
1987	75.3
1992	77.7
1997	71.4
2001	59.4
2005	61.4

Vox Pops

Nothing will do more damage to the pro-European movement than giving room to the suspicion that we have something to hide, that we do not have the cojones *to carry our argument to the people.*

Nick Clegg MP (Sheffield Hallam), Liberal Democrat leader and polyglot

I understand that cojones *is Spanish for a rude word. That demonstrates to me that the Liberal Democrats can talk balls in many languages – and, indeed, frequently do so.*

Ian Davidson MP (Labour, Glasgow South West), gets his claws out in response

A Political Devil's Dictionary

Anybody who is in a position to serve this country ought to understand the consequences of words.
George W. Bush, US president 2001–09

Anarchy

Not, as one might surmise from the work of the Sex Pistols, a dedication to destruction and chaos. The association with vibrant (even violent) disorder has passed into popular usage, the word immediately bringing associations to mind, depending on one's age, with the demonstrations of 1968, the early 1980s urban riots, the poll tax riots of 1990, or the May Day protests of recent years. Literally speaking, the word (from the Greek) means 'without government'. In its purest sense, it is a theoretical social state in which there is no governing person or body, but in which the individual has absolute liberty. Whether this would actually work in practice is, of course, the subject of endless debate. And not just by age-ing punks. One of the traditional symbols of anarchy, we note in passing, is the black flag. Surely every anarchist should have his *own* flag? Or the right not to carry a flag at all?

Annihilation

Those of us who were teenagers in the 1980s were always quite convinced that we were going to die in a nuclear explosion some time in the following week, especially as we had grown up with *Protect and Survive* information films, the grim drama *Threads* and constant controversies

over American airbases in Britain. We were convinced
that Ronnie Reagan meant it about fighting a 'limited
nuclear war in Europe', and that his trembly old finger
was poised over the button, ready to wipe out the Evil
Empire, with us caught in the crossfire. Today, you're
more likely to hear the word in connection with climate
change – or a wipe-out in the polls.

Antipathy

Most people don't really *like* politicians very much.
Former Conservative leader Iain Duncan Smith famously
said to David Dimbleby, in the wake of the expenses
fiasco, that politicians' reputations had sunk 'almost as
low as that of journalists'. So anyone going into politics
already has a hill to climb.

Don't assume your would-be MP is a deceitful slyboots
until you have actual evidence – they are just as likely
(in fact, more likely) to be someone who really wants to
make a difference, who doesn't necessarily agree with
every dotted I and crossed T of their party's manifesto,
and who will have put in an awful lot of groundwork as
a councillor or party activist over the years. After all, you
may find yourself coming to him or her for support when
your child can't get a school place or the council threat-
ens to build a sixteen-storey concrete monstrosity on the
site of your favourite local nature reserve. And if you have
shaken your fist at them on the doorstep and called them
a money-grabbing cad, they may just remember. And tell
you where to stick your vote.

Apathy

The thing they – and we – are trying to overcome.
Some university students think it is terribly amusing

and original to have an 'Apathy Party' alongside all the political stalls at Freshers' Fair. One assumes they have to disband if anybody shows any interest in coming to meetings. People are still notoriously bad at turning out for elections, to the extent where the 2008 Haltemprice and Howden by-election (the one where former shadow home secretary David Davis resigned and got re-elected) had a turnout of 35 per cent, and this was somehow seen as good. This was despite the same by-election having given the good denizens of Haltemprice and Howden the opportunity to vote for Miss Great Britain, and to make predictable sexist jokes.

Basics
What we were supposed to be getting back to, according to an ill-fated announcement by the John Major government of the 1990s. Somewhat undermined by a succession of sexual scandals to hit Tory ministers. There was never really a consensus as to what these 'basics' were, but one suspects the phrase was designed to appeal to the readers of certain newspapers. See also **family values**.

Ballot box
Symbol of democracy – the receptacle into which your ballot slip is placed. Some constituencies have taken to having brand new tamper-proof ballot boxes in their polling stations, which are yellow and black with a fierce-looking zip and padlock, and look like the kind of implement one might find in a 'specialist publication'. Other new models are made of clear plastic. In 1872, the first secret ballot to elect an MP in the northern hemisphere was held, and the system we now all know well – marking

an X on the paper and placing it in the box (originally a wooden container sealed with wax) – was born.

BBC
Iconic symbol of Britain, broadcaster respected throughout the world – and often accused of left-wing tendencies. Controversies aside, the corporation is closely watched by MPs for any sign of bias.

By-election
Meaningless distraction, or taking of the political temperature? A by-election is a vote in a constituency which has become vacant, which the media and all parties concerned will try to get terribly excited about. Camera crews will stop Mrs Edna Bigott in the local high street, find out that she is voting BNP as she wants to send home all those 'what don't belong here', and will then produce a colour bar chart extrapolating Edna's vote to a general election in which the BNP take all 646 seats with a huge majority. Not really, but it's almost as silly as what they actually do.

By-elections are 'safe' – they're a place for the bloody-nosers (see chapter 1) to have a good thump without actually worrying about who or what they might have inadvertently voted into office. They also offer an opportunity for politicians to pursue more limited agendas than they otherwise would – the most prominent example in recent years being former shadow home secretary David Davis's decision (which some found bewildering) to stand down from the opposition front bench and from his seat, and to fight a by-election on the issue of 42-day detention for terror suspects. Thanks to this, we were treated to the thoughtful musings of Gemma Garrett from the Miss Great Britain party on issues of national security, and the profound and rigorous debate of Mad Cow-Girl from the Monster Raving Loony Party about ID cards.

The entire focus of a party's campaigning time and resources ends up being channelled into a little place many may not have heard of. Inevitably, by-elections are given greater media exposure than they perhaps deserve, and are jumped upon by the media as temperature-taking polls on the government of the time. Even with all of this in mind, milestone by-elections are still interesting in retrospect – such as Newbury, which in 1993 saw a swing to the Liberal Democrats of 23 per cent, and which was the first of a succession of defeats for John Major's government. The swing to the Conservatives at Crewe and Nantwich in 2008 may come to be regarded as a similarly significant marker. So watch them closely – but we'll forgive you if you don't stay up until 2.00am to see the live results.

Chattering classes
Those who discuss politics and the issues of the day over their dinner tables, and to whom politicians are often accused of trying to appeal. Those who discuss the same issues by updating their online status every five minutes are presumably the 'Twittering classes'.

Choice
Theoretical policy of ensuring that parents are able to send their children to the schools they want. In practice, means having to send children to the school the government wants *for* them. Rather misses the point that most parents don't want 'choice' – they just want a good

school on their doorstep. The cynical claim this is never going to happen, because some rubbish state schools are needed in order to make the great many average ones look good.

Confidentiality
Hiding things from the voters which they would find it quite interesting or useful to know. Such as how much you spent on your duck house, or on having meals twice in two separate places at the same time. (Are MPs possessed of more than one stomach, like the fictional cat Six Dinner Sid, or Paul Gascoigne's legendary friend Jimmy 'Five Bellies'?)

conservative (small c)
A liberal who has been mugged.

Constituency
Area represented by an MP, and where they usually spend Fridays and at least part of the weekend. It usually helps to live there if you want to be elected – great capital has been known to be made out of aspiring MPs who have been 'parachuted' in (although not literally, in some kind of Michael Portillo/SAS-style dawn raid), or who have committed the heinous crime of living a few hundred yards outside the constituency boundary where the nicer schools – or more 'appropriate' schools – and lower levels of crime are to be found. Some of them are very good at running regular 'surgeries' where they deal with constituents' problems: everything from the holes in the road to the state of the hospitals.

Credit crunch

Supposedly going to be over by the end of 2010, 2012 or 2015, depending on who you believe and how you define 'over'.

Crisis

Always good for testing a politician's mettle. Jim Callaghan stepped off the plane and declared that the unrest of 1978–9 was exaggerated, which led to the famous mis-quote: 'Crisis? What Crisis?' Thirty years later, Gordon Brown faced a similar scenario, increasingly unpopular and being accused in the media of indifference to rising fuel and food costs and the downward-spiralling housing market. His ten years of stalwart prudence as chancellor now seemed to count for nothing, and everyone soon forgot the first three months of media fawning after his 'firefighting' of foot and mouth, terrorist threats and floods. Tony Blair, on the other hand, looked at his most statesmanlike when speaking to the country after the 7 July 2005 bombings, and seemed to pitch his response well by coming down to London from the G8 summit in Gleneagles, then returning to Scotland to finish the business there.

Death

Always unfortunate as a career move in politics, but likely to result in one's opponents speaking rather more highly of you than they did when facing you across the Chamber or the *Newsnight* studio. The most memorable piece of political clog-popping in recent years has to be that of Labour's leader John Smith, widely expected to take the party to an election victory in 1994, and to whom tributes were paid in a pin-droppingly quiet Commons.

Former foreign secretary Robin Cook, who died in 2005, also invited colourful tributes from all sides, some for his stand against the Iraq war. Seven UK prime ministers have died in office – Spencer Compton, 1st Earl of Wilmington (in 1743), Henry Pelham (1745), Charles Watson-Wentworth, 2nd Marquess of Rockingham (1782), William Pitt the Younger (1806), Spencer Perceval (1812), George Canning (1827) and Henry Temple, 3rd Viscount Palmerston (1865). Of those, Spencer Perceval was the only one careless enough to get himself assassinated. One would in the past have added 'as every schoolboy knows' to that sentence, but these days one really can't take anything for granted.

Deceit
Imaginative use of the facts, of which political parties constantly suspect one another but of which they are not actually allowed to accuse one another, at least not in the Commons itself. It seems to be the voters' general, resigned assumption that most politicians are into this.

Decency
A much-sought-after quality in one's political opponents. Always easier to praise them for it when they are on the way out. Some people's political antennae are still buzzing with 'does not compute' messages at the memory of David Cameron and the Tories leading the standing ovation for the outgoing Tony Blair in June 2007.

Defence policy
The various ways and means, and provision of equipment, for wiping out one's fellow human beings.

Deprived area

Shorthand for anywhere which doesn't have leafy lanes or a nice delicatessen. More technically, one which scores highly on the Indices of Deprivation, which monitor housing, education, crime and so on. Politicians of all colours claim to want to eradicate this, but secretly wonder whether it might not be a good idea to have a little, otherwise the people in the nice houses will feel they have wasted their big mortgages.

Electability

The art of pleasing all of the people all of the time. After losing four successive elections, the Labour party was starting to wonder if they would ever have it again. But the process of restructuring had already begun under Neil Kinnock and under the mediagenic Tony Blair it was to continue – abandoning, some said, everything that made them Labour in the first place. A difficult balancing act – without being in power, you can't do anything, but how do you get into power if people don't like what you're offering?

Election

That awkward time when the parties have to let the people have their say about the issues of the day. Sometimes milestones in history, other times damp squibs.

Family values

Occasionally invoked, but never properly defined, when seeking the votes of Middle England. Would appear, on the surface, to be the kind of thing which will appeal to *Daily Mail*-reading, homeowning voters.

Filibustering

Extending a debate in order to delay taking a vote on a Bill. Many politicians are adept at this – it basically involves their waffling on for extended periods without being interrupted, so it often comes naturally to them.

Government

Plenty of different forms have been tried. Despite the expense and the bureaucracy, democracy still seems as if it is the least worst for now. Revolutions often end up with things going back to the way they were after a while, civil wars are usually messy, and forced regime change requires a great deal of persuasion and, let's face it, military might.

Grass roots

Support for an issue at a fundamental level, something which politicians like to demonstrate is in evidence if they want to get an idea off the ground. These days, the internet allows for the more sneaky practice of **astroturfing**, which is (obviously, when one thinks about it) fake grass-roots support.

Interview

For the politician, he or she hopes, a nice cosy chat in which he or she gets to talk in a relaxed way about some nice policies they want to introduce which are going to make the country into a land of milk and honey. For the interviewer, especially if it's Jeremy Paxman or John Humphrys, it's a chance to bare the teeth, unsheathe the claws and eviscerate every last shoddy, ill-conceived, half-baked idea they've come armed with, plus a few more they hadn't thought of. No surprise that the average political leader prefers a nice chat on the sofa with the likes of Fern Britton. Ironically, the most tenacious interviewer of Margaret 'just let me finish' Thatcher, and the only one to look as if she had actually rattled her, was not a professional at all, but a member of the public, Diana Gould, who had Maggie on the ropes with Paxo-like tenacity over the sinking of the Argentine warship *General Belgrano* in 1982. Michael Howard once famously faced the same question from Jeremy Paxman fourteen times – a tactic which, it was revealed in a later discussion between the two men, came about not through dogged journalistic tenacity but because Paxman's producer had told him through his earpiece that another item had been delayed and he had a few more minutes to fill.

Issue

Anything a politician wishes to talk about. Pronounced *issss-ew* (in Brian Sewell mode) or *ish-ooo* (in the manner of, say, Kerry Katona), depending on whether they are on Radio 4 or visiting a young people's housing project at the time. Politicians like to set the agenda themselves, and get irritated at being put on the back foot by their opponents.

Jeopardy

That which activates politicians' minds around election time – also known as 'fear of losing your seat'. Manifests itself as sudden, urgent visibility in the media.

Kip

A bit of shut-eye. Does politics send you to sleep? It would appear so, given the number of MPs one sees snoozing, even on the front benches. Margaret Thatcher famously got by on four hours' sleep a night – so, apparently, does Barack Obama. Maybe we should be worried about this.

Knives
Metaphorically, a useful tool for getting on in one's political career. In the literal sense, a much-touted example of the crime and disorder on our streets.

liberal (small l)
A conservative who has been imprisoned.

Listening
What governments always say they are going to do after a major election cock-up. An attempt to inject a little humility into the proceedings, usually forgotten a few weeks later.

Manifesto
Glossy document laying out in detail – or, sometimes, in annoyingly vague terms – what the party concerned aims to do once it gets into government. Sometimes these can be hugely amusing, as you can find yourself throwing up your hands halfway through, skimming it across the room and screaming: 'Where's the *money* going to come from for all this?' (The usual answer being 'you, the taxpayer'.) Manifestos should be treated not as some kind of holy writ or stone-carved tablet, but as a sort of 'lesson plan' which will be riffed upon, adapted or possibly even discarded entirely as the realities of government hit home. Some argue that part of the problem we have now, in the current cycle of multi-term governments which has been going on since 1979, is that entire generations of politicians grow up occupying one shadow

position after another, and that they are not prepared to make the kind of reluctant concessions which make their manifestos look more realistic. Tony Blair was propelled into the job of prime minister without having held any other government job; David Cameron looks to be heading the same way.

Party political broadcast
Pieces of social satire and five-minute sitcoms which pepper the TV schedules at election time. Used to feature a party leader in 'serious mode' at a desk addressing the nation, but have since become glossy video brochures which sometimes go as long as they can without mentioning politics or the party name at all. Often ask leading questions: 'Do you want to live in a Britain where you step outside your door and are beset by a gang of violent knife-wielding hoodies? No, nor do we.'

Political correctness (gone mad)
The correct response by a right-winger to any 'loony left' initiative, usually reported by the *Daily Mail* and stoked up out of all proportion. Usually refers to the nation's schoolchildren being taught to sing 'Baa Baa Green Sheep', or some such fictional idiocy. Used less these days since the phrase was mercilessly parodied by the 'Tory Wives' sketch in *Spitting Image*.

Polling station
Church halls, school halls, even temporary shacks erected on roundabouts – all of these can act as the place one casts one's vote on polling day. There is something terribly satisfying, old-fashioned and British about going along and marking a cross on a piece of paper with a

pencil tied to a rickety wooden booth. Will successive governments resist the temptation to make the process more hi-tech? An electronic system surely can't be safeguarded against abuse, which is one of the best reasons for keeping pencil and paper.

Popularity

Courted by politicians of all colours, as they know that the people they represent have the power to kick them out of their jobs in a few years' time. Of course, this does not stop them from taking unpopular decisions.

Quango

Quasi-Autonomous Non-Governmental Organisation. People tend to hate them instinctively without knowing much about them. Officially, they don't exist. Unofficially, they carry on the business of public administration without political interference.

Rabid

Necessary adjective for any strongly left- or right-of-centre view with which the speaker does not agree. Sometimes accompanied by 'rampantly', or 'foaming at the mouth'.

Recession

Two consecutive quarters of negative economic growth, as seen in the early 1990s and in 2008/09 and possibly beyond. It probably doesn't do to make grandiose statements about there being 'no return to boom and bust', given that this sort of thing seems inevitable from time to time. And when the jury is out on how long a recession will last, announcing strategies to cope with it after the event is not as good as prevention, but is at least better than pretending it isn't really happening or that it isn't as bad as the media claim.

Recount

Desperate attempt to delay the inevitable when a party looks as if they have lost a seat by ten votes, and their candidate is gnawing his knuckles, thumping the bar and spitting his teeth left, right and centre as he wishes he'd gone and dragged the Fotherington-Thomas family, including eighteen-year-old Tarquin who's home from university, away from their game of cribbage and driven them down to the polling station to vote.

Silent majority

The funny thing about silent majorities is that they are always fairly talkative. Turn on any radio talk show and the chances are you'll hear a self-defined member of one, usually foaming at the mouth about immigrants, cyclists, benefit scroungers or whatever else has rattled their cage that day. At some point, they will use the words: 'I pay my taxes.'

Sock-puppetry

The art of creating personae for oneself on internet forums, in order to give the illusion of multiple voices supporting a point of view – when in reality they are all you. See also **astroturfing** (under **grass roots**).

Stalking horse

Like the canary in the mine, the stalking horse is sent in first to sniff the political air. Sir Anthony Meyer secured his place in the history books by being the first stalking horse for Margaret Thatcher, but perhaps the most famous – although he never intended to be one – was Michael Heseltine, to whom the famous expression 'He who wields the knife never wears the crown' is attributed.

Thatcherism

We have said enough about Margaret, but it's worth noting that politicians from all ends of the spectrum still seem haunted by her ideology – and less sure of themselves now she has gone. Those on the Left had a convenient, easily identifiable hate figure during the 1980s and much of the 1990s. Now, the political divisions are less clear. We head forward into a time without such clear 'isms', and maybe British politics is all the more interesting for it.

Think tanks

Independent bodies whose job it is to 'think the unthinkable' in order to help parties to formulate policies. Sometimes it's not just the unthinkable but the downright daft. The parties won't necessarily take on everything the think tanks come up with – they'd be roasted alive if they took them all seriously.

Today

Radio 4's early morning current affairs programme. Simultaneously respected and feared, the essential but terrifying arena in which politicians can make their views known to Middle England. The presenters are adept at sticking the knife in at just the right moment, skewering some unfortunate politician who has not even had his breakfast yet – it's even more amusing when you picture the scene, because they are probably squirming in their dressing gown in the BBC radio car parked outside their house.

Yoof

Young persons, also known as potential voters. Politicians seem anxious to court the 'youth vote' – no coincidence that all three main parties have, in the last decade, been led by a youngish, photogenic chap who at least gives the impression of knowing an iPod from a Walkman, and is vaguely aware that the Arctic Monkeys are not something discovered by David Attenborough. But does anybody seriously believe that the rowdy Sheffield foursome are really Gordon Brown's choice of morning listening? David Cameron went out of his way to woo the thirty-somethings with his love of The Smiths, spinning his student days as having been spent unloved and listening to Morrissey in a bedsit rather than out causing havoc with the Bullingdon Club ... Young people, it's fair to say, are probably not impressed by such gimmicks. After all, when you're eighteen, a 40-year-old chap in a suit looks much like a 55-year-old chap in a suit, tie or no tie – and they'd probably much rather be reassured that the guy in charge is going to provide them with some hope of education, training and employment rather than owning an entire download of *The Queen Is Dead*.

Zero tolerance

Depending on which end of the political spectrum you come from, this is either the answer to all crimes and misdemeanours or the beginning of a totalitarian state. New York Mayor Rudy Giuliani adopted it as a policy – working on the principle that clamping down on the 'little' wrongdoings would help keep the bigger crime waves at bay. Overall crime rates in the city dropped by 44 per cent, the murder rate by 70 per cent. Those are the kind of statistics UK home secretaries dream of (or make up).

Zzzzzzz ...

So, does politics still send you to sleep? One hopes not. Even if only one thing in this book has seized your interest or imagination, it may have encouraged you to go away and become involved in the political process: by running a local grass roots campaign, standing for the parish or borough council, lobbying your MP, joining a pressure group or writing to a politician about a subject close to your heart. Politics is you. You are politics. Go out there and make it happen.

Highly Selective Bibliography

This is by no means the kind of exhaustive bibliography one finds in more serious political tomes – it's just an indication of a few of the books I've found useful or entertaining in the compiling of this book, and which you may too.

Terry Arthur, *Crap: A Guide to Politics* (Continuum International Publishing Group Ltd., 2007)

Martin Bell, *The Truth That Sticks: New Labour's Breach of Trust* (Icon Books Ltd, 2008)

Duncan Brack and Iain Dale (eds.), *Prime Minister Portillo: And Other Things That Never Happened* (Politico's Publishing, 2004)

Alastair Campbell, *The Blair Years* (Arrow Books, 2008)

Robert Eccleshall and Graham Walker (eds.), *Biographical Dictionary of British Prime Ministers* (Routledge, 1998)

James Harkin, *Big Ideas: The Essential Guide to the Latest Thinking* (Atlantic Books, 2008)

Simon Hoggart, *The Hands of History: Parliamentary Sketches 1997–2007* (Guardian Books, 2007)

Gerald Kaufman, *How To Be A Minister* (Sidgwick and Jackson, 1980, 1997)

David Laws and Paul Marshall (eds.), *The Orange Book: Reclaiming Liberalism* (Profile Books, 2004)

Michael Moore, *Mike's Election Guide* (Penguin, 2008)

Jo-Anne Nadler, *Too Nice To Be A Tory: It's My Party and I'll Cry If I Want To* (Simon and Schuster, 2004)

John O'Farrell, *Things Can Only Get Better: Eighteen
    Miserable Years in the Life of a Labour Supporter, 1979–
    1997* (Black Swan, 1999)

Matthew Parris and Kevin Maguire, *Great Parliamentary
    Scandals: Five Centuries of Calumny, Smear and
    Innuendo* (Robson Books Ltd., 2004)

Matthew Parris, *Off-Message: New Labour, New Sketches*
    (Robson Books, 2001)

Ed Rayner and Ron Stapley, *Debunking History: 152
    Popular Myths Exploded* (The History Press Ltd.,
    2006)

Margaret Thatcher, *The Downing Street Years*
    (HarperCollins, 1993)

Margaret Thatcher, *The Path To Power* (HarperCollins,
    1995)

Geoffrey Wheatcroft, *The Strange Death of Tory England*
    (Penguin, 2005)

Even More Selective Guide to Websites

Bear in mind that this is just a starter's guide and will
barely scratch the surface. To list all the useful politics-
related websites out there would take up an entire book
on its own!

* For regular updates on what's happening in the
  political world, you can't beat the BBC News at
  http://news.bbc.co.uk/1/hi/uk_politics, while the
  online home of *Total Politics* magazine at www.
  totalpolitics.com is magnificently wide-ranging. Also
  see the *Spectator* magazine at www.spectator.co.uk,

and browse the blog at www.spectator.co.uk/coffee house as well. Politics Home at www.politicshome. com is almost too busy to get your head around, but it repays investigation.

- The major serious newspaper sites are always useful, of course: try www.guardian.co.uk/politics, www.independent.co.uk/news/uk/politics and www. timesonline.co.uk/tol/news/politics to start you off.

- Have a look at www.epolitix.com for news, press reviews, podcasts and much more. While if it's irreverence you're after, you'll find it aplenty at www. private-eye.co.uk for the UK variety, and www. theonion.com for US-centric humour.

- For right-of-centre voices, a good place to start is Conservative Home, http://conservativehome. blogs.com/, written by former Conservative Central Office staffer Tim Montgomerie. Then the best-known blogs on that side of the fence belong to Iain Dale and Guido Fawkes: www.iaindale.blogspot. com and www.order-order.com respectively. At www. conservatives.com/News/Blogs.aspx you will find the Conservatives' newly-launched Blue Blog.

- For the left side of the political fence, try Recess Monkey at www.recessmonkey.com and Tom Watson at www.tom-watson.co.uk, and for a multi-authored 'liberal left' blog try Liberal Conspiracy at www. liberalconspiracy.org as well. If you like your Leftism a little harder, then get yourself over to Lenin's Tomb at http://leninology.blogspot.com or Ian Bone at http://ianbone.wordpress.com

- In the centre ground, Lib Dem Voice at http://
  www.libdemvoice.org is an independent blog run by
  Liberal Democrat activists, and it's also worth looking at Lincoln councillor Ryan Cullen's http://www.
  libdemblogs.co.uk, which collects the best from
  around the Liberal Democrat blogosphere. The Hug
  A Hoodie blog at http://hugahoodie.blogspot.com
  is also enjoyably outspoken.

- For Green issues, try the obvious, Greenpeace at
  http://www.greenpeace.org.uk/blog, plus Hippy
  Shopper at www.hippyshopper.com for a bit of 'ethi-
  cal consumerism'.

- It's well worth taking a look at the interviews and
  discussions on the 18 Doughty Street channel at
  http://18doughtystreet.blip.tv (now archive-only),
  while Catch 21 Productions is a site run by and
  for young people and based at Westminster – go to
  www.catch21.co.uk to check it out.

- Now for some sites to help you become a more
  active citizen. You can find MPs' contact details at
  www.parliament.uk/directories/hciolists/alms.cfm
  and also at the *Guardian*'s listing, http://politics.
  guardian.co.uk/person/browse/mps/az, or you
  can also look at www.theyworkforyou.com or www.
  writetothem.com, both of which offer the facility to
  email or fax your MP.

- You could try some basic stuff on parties and policies at www.how2vote.co.uk/sections.php if you feel
  so inclined. And find out where you stand politically by taking the political survey at www.political
  survey2005.com or trying the Political Compass at

www.politicalcompass.org, both of which will ask various questions of you and plot your results on a graph. A click on www.electoral-reform.org.uk will take you to the home of the Electoral Reform Society.

- Intriguing speculation and amusing (but informed) prediction can be found at the home of Electoral Calculus at www.electoralcalculus.co.uk, while Political Betting at http://politicalbetting.com gives you the latest odds and polls, and analysis of the stories behind them.

- And finally, if you feel really enthused, you may like to pop over to the UK Politics Forum at www.politicsforum.co.uk/forum, either for a browse or to contribute.

Happy browsing!